NOODLES
ASIAN STYLE

CARA HOBDAY

PHOTOGRAPHS BY
ROBIN MATTHEWS

NEW YORK

CONTENTS

THE CUPBOARD

Oriental food is now so popular that it is increasingly easy to buy the ingredients that provide the intriguing exotic flavors.
Of course, not everyone lives near Chinese or Japanese grocery stores, but a well-stocked supermarket will sell most of the ingredients
required for the recipes in this book. Health food stores are another excellent source of nuts, seeds, and Japanese ingredients.

Flavorings Coconut milk, very rich, sold in cans or as a powder; dried bonito (tuna) flakes, widely used in Japanese cooking; dried shrimp, usually soaked before use, pinker ones are generally fresher; kamaboko (also spelled namaboko) and naruto, dried Japanese fishcakes; mirin, Japanese sweetened rice wine; miso, soybean paste with a wonderful deep flavor; red curry paste, hot Thai flavoring sold in jars or plastic containers; rice wine, Chinese shaoxing and Japanese sake are very different, but dry sherry can be used instead; shrimp paste (also known as blachan with various spellings), made from salted, fermented shrimp, is used sparingly to add a pungent, savory flavor—keep it well-wrapped in the refrigerator; wasabi, Japanese horseradish, is less hot and pungent than Western horseradish, and is sold as a powder or paste.

Tamarind is an acidic fruit, widely used in Asian cooking to add a refreshing, sour taste to dishes. It is sold as a ready-to-use paste or dried in blocks. To extract tamarind juice from dried tamarind pulp, mix 2 tablespoons pulp with 4 tablespoons water and push through a strainer. For a stronger flavor, leave to soak for 1 to 2 hours before straining.

Herbs and spices Basil, always used fresh (red basil has a more subtle flavor than green basil); chilies, used fresh or dried, whole or in flakes; cilantro—bunches of fresh leaves and stems have a very different flavor from the round brown seeds; galangal—looks similar to ginger and has a subtle flavor; garlic; garlic chives, which look like large chives, but have a garlic flavor; gingerroot—buy fresh, firm, smooth knobs of ginger— usually peeled, then grated, sliced, or shredded; kaffir lime leaves have a citrus aroma, available dried or fresh (keep fresh leaves in the freezer); lemongrass has a subtle lemon flavor (fresh is far superior to dried; remove the tough outer leaves and use the tender core); peppercorns—black, white, green, and the reddish-brown Sichuan peppercorns (also known as aromatic pepper) all have different flavors; seven-pepper spice, or Japanese pepper, is a blend of spices, including chilies, sesame, white pepper, nori, and dried orange peel; lemon pepper can be used instead of seven-pepper spice; onion pepper is another aromatic spice blend; star anise is a beautiful star-shaped seed pod with a distinctive and aromatic flavor—use whole or extract the seeds; turmeric, usually bought as a powder, adds a bright yellow color and slightly bitter flavor, which is often used to balance sweetness.

Nuts and seeds These add a crunchy texture to stir-fries, and are sometimes served separately, as garnishes—cashew nuts, natural (unsalted) peanuts, sesame seeds, sunflower seeds.

Oils and vinegars Chili oil is used as a flavoring; groundnut, or peanut, oil has a neutral flavor and is very good for the high temperatures needed for deep-frying; sesame oil has a rich, strong, nutty taste, and can be used, sparingly, for frying or as a flavoring; sunflower oil is an excellent all-purpose cooking oil.

Wine vinegar and garlic vinegar have a place in the Oriental kitchen, but most common is rice vinegar, made from fermented rice. Cider vinegar can be used in place of white rice vinegar. Chinese black rice vinegar has a rich taste, somewhat like Italian balsamic vinegar.

Pickles Pickled Chinese cabbage and pickled radish are often used in stir-fries; pickled ginger is sold sliced or shredded—the shredded version is pink, and is most often used as a garnish.

Sauce: Bean sauce or paste is a thick, salty, aromatic condiment made from soybeans; it may be black or yellow. Fish sauce (called *nam pla* in Thailand and *nuoc mam* in Vietnam), made from salted and fermented fish, is a very pungent, clear brown liquid; it loses a lot of its "punch" and fishiness when heated. Hoisin sauce is a dark brown, sweet, and spicy sauce made from soybeans. Oyster sauce is thick, rich, and savory. Soy sauce varies from country to country: China has light and dark versions, both saltier than the Japanese; *kecap manis* is dark, sweet, Indonesian soy sauce.

Sea vegetables Sold dried and usually used as flavorings or garnishes. They can be reconstituted quickly in water. Hijiki is black, and sold in pieces; konbu (also spelled kombu), similar to kelp, is used to make dashi broth; nori, similar to laver, is sold in paper-thin, purple-black sheets, and is often toasted and then flaked; wakame is dark green. Dashi broth, the base of many Asian dishes, is sold in instant form.

Vegetables (canned and dried) Usually added to dishes for their texture. Bamboo shoots are pale yellow and crunchy; Chinese dried mushrooms have an intense flavor and chewy texture—to reconstitute, soak in warm water for about 20 minutes or until soft, then drain and squeeze dry, discard the hard stems and use only the caps; straw mushrooms have a very mild flavor and soft texture, sold in cans; water chestnuts are white and very crisp, usually sold peeled in cans.

TYPES OF NOODLES

In almost all of the recipes in this book, the noodles are interchangeable, so you can use whichever is your favorite type. If you see any Japanese noodles that seem to be outrageously priced, they are probably te'uchi, *or hand-made.*

Beancurd noodles *(also called transparent noodles, cellophane noodles)*: These are fine vermicelli noodles. These come tied in a bundle—either a large bundle, or a smaller bundle for one portion. The packages may be marked "beanthread," "peastarch," or "beanstarch." Because of the processes used to make them, it is very difficult to separate the noodles when they are dry, which is why they are often sold in single-portion bundles. If the noodles are to be used to make a stuffing, they will have to be broken up after cooking. Beancurd noodles have a beautiful translucent appearance to them once they are cooked, and they do not stick together, so they are useful in stir-fries and salads.

Chinese wheat noodles *(ho fen)* These are flat, sticklike noodles. They have a heavy texture, and are great with vegetarian dishes or dishes with a lot of sauce. Flat rice noodles make good substitutes.

Chow mein noodles Designed to hold chow mein sauce, these are thin, flat egg noodles. Medium egg noodles can be used instead.

Egg noodles Made from wheat flour, eggs, and water, these are sold in thread (fine) or medium thicknesses. These noodles are readily available and very popular. Egg noodles do not stick when stir-fried, are satisfying as an accompaniment, and absorb dressings easily, all of which makes them versatile and easy to work with. They can also be deep-fried very successfully.

Mie noodles Nests of Chinese egg noodles, made to a slightly less rich recipe than egg noodles. They are also available with chili flavoring.

Ramen noodles Crinkly Japanese noodles, these are available fresh or dried. They are often sold as instant meals, with an envelope of flavored soup in the package with the noodles. They are very cheap, so discard the envelopes of flavoring and use the noodles. Ramen noodles are usually used in a soup-stew, a nutritious and filling one-pot meal.

Rice noodles Chinese noodles made from rice flour and water, these are available as vermicelli, in thread (fine) thickness or flat, when they are sometimes called rice sticks. These are recognizable by their white color and translucence, both when raw and cooked. They are easily confused with beancurd noodles, so look for the word "rice" or "riz" on the package. Rice noodles have a bland flavor, which makes them ideal as an accompaniment for highly flavored or rich dishes. Thread or fine rice noodles are ideal chopped and used as a stuffing or in a stir-fry. All rice noodles are great deep-fried.

Soba noodles These are Japanese thin noodles, made from varying percentages of buckwheat flour. The more buckwheat they contain, the better they are (and the more expensive). Noodles with a buckwheat content of 40 percent are a good choice, and reasonably priced. These noodles may be brown or green, so they add color to salads or stir-fries. Soba noodles are quite filling, so they are usually served in smaller portions than other noodles.

Somen noodles Use these thin, very fine Japanes wheatflour noodles for stir-fries, in soups, and as accompaniments. They are also sold in rainbow colors to use in salads, which look attractive on the serving dish. They can be used as a substitute for udon noodles.

Udon noodles Japanese, very narrow, ribbonlike, wheatflour noodles, these are available fresh or dried. The dried version is slightly flatter than the fresh. These noodles have a satisfying texture and chewability, and are excellent stir-fried, or used to make a satisfying soup-stew.

COOKING NOODLES SUCCESSFULLY

When cooking noodles, bear in mind what they will be used for. Noodles that will be in a soupy dish need to be slightly undercooked so they do not fall apart, whereas noodles that are to be stir-fried should be cooked in plenty of boiling water, to disperse the starch content. (It is the starch in the noodles that makes them stick together during cooking.)

Cook noodles as soon as possible before they are to be served. This is especially important for flat rice noodles, which often stick together.

There are basically two ways to cook noodles. The first is suitable for particularly fine noodles, such as beancurd noodles, rice vermicelli, or egg thread noodles, as well as for nest noodles so they keep their shape. Put the noodles into a very large heatproof bowl and pour in plenty of boiling water. Let the noodles stand for the time suggested on the package, then drain them in a colander before using.

The second method, which should be used for larger dried noodles, is to plunge the noodles into a large pan of boiling water (use the biggest pan available, as you cannot have too much water to cook noodles). When a white foam—the starch from the noodles—rises to the surface, add a cup of cold water to the pan. When the water returns to a boil, add another cup of cold water. Some noodles will be cooked when the water boils for the third time, while others will need one more addition of cold water. The cold water ensures that the surface of the noodle does not break up and become "furry," giving out more starch and spoiling your recipe. Drain and rinse the noodles before using.

THE RECIPES

NOODLES TO START

Fragrant noodle soups are a feature of many Asian cuisines, either as a delicate first course or as a sustaining snack enjoyed at any time of day. Other appetizers use noodles in ingenious ways—as a stuffing for artichokes, a filling for egg rolls, or as the base for crabcakes. All recipes in this chapter serve 4 to 6, unless otherwise indicated.

HOT-AND-SOUR SOUP

This soup is sold on street corners all over Southeast Asia by mobile food vendors. They carry with them everything they need to make their particular specialty—wok, burner, ingredients—balanced in panniers across their shoulders. The soup is whipped up in a flash, and it is up to the customer to say how much or how little chili he wants.

7 ounces egg thread noodles
1 tablespoon sunflower oil
Generous 1 cup sliced shiitake mushrooms

2 tablespoons chopped fresh cilantro
Salt
1 1/2 bunches (4 oz) watercress

FOR THE STOCK
1 tablespoon tamarind pulp (page 5)
2 dried red chilies
2 kaffir lime leaves
1-inch piece gingerroot, chopped

2-inch piece galangal, chopped
1 stalk lemongrass, chopped
1 onion, quartered
4 1/2 cups water

TO GARNISH
1 fresh red chili, thinly sliced
Lime wedges

Bean sprouts

Put all the ingredients for the stock into a saucepan and bring to a boil. Simmer for 5 minutes. Strain.

Return the stock to the saucepan and bring back to a boil. Add the noodles and cook for 3 minutes. Using tongs or a slotted spoon, remove the noodles from the stock and divide between the serving bowls. Reserve the stock.

Heat the oil in a wok or large skillet and cook the sliced mushrooms over high heat for 1 minute or until they have softened. Add the stock and stir in the chopped cilantro. Add salt to taste.

Divide the watercress between the serving bowls and ladle the soup over the noodles and watercress. Garnish each bowl with a couple of red chili slices. Serve hot, with lime wedges and bean sprouts.

STUFFED LOTUS LEAVES

Lotus leaves and banana leaves are sold in most Oriental supermarkets. Using leaves as a wrapping keeps all the moisture and flavors in the stuffing, and the bundles look exotic and impressive.

Makes 4 bundles

8 lotus leaves or banana leaves, washed and cut into 8-inch squares
3 1/2 ounces beancurd noodles
6 ounces white fish fillet
1 tablespoon red curry paste
3 shallots, finely chopped
3 scallions, finely chopped
Juice of 1 lime
1 teaspoon turmeric

1/2 teaspoon crushed garlic
2 teaspoons fish sauce
1 teaspoon white peppercorns, crushed
2 fresh red chilies, seeded and chopped
Scant 1/2 cup coconut milk
About 1 tablespoon Indonesian soy sauce (kecap manis), plus extra for serving
1 egg, lightly beaten
Bottled chili sauce, to serve

Soak the lotus leaves in warm water for about 10 minutes to soften. Blanch the lotus or banana leaves in boiling water for 6 minutes. Drain, refresh under cold running water, and leave to drain.

Cook the noodles in plenty of boiling water for 3 minutes or according to the package directions. Drain and snip them into pieces.

Put the fish fillet into a food processor and process until finely chopped. Alternatively, finely chop it by hand. Add the red curry paste, shallots, scallions, lime juice, turmeric, crushed garlic, fish sauce, white pepper, and red chilies. Process or mash until fairly smooth. Stir in the coconut milk. Season to taste with *kecap manis*, and stir in the egg and the noodles.

Flatten 4 of the lotus leaves, or banana leaves, on the countertop. Divide the fish stuffing between the leaves and fold each leaf neatly around the stuffing. If you are using banana leaves, it may be easiest to make a pleat along each side and fold in the edges, or to wrap up like a present. Fold another leaf neatly around the first leaf to enclose the filling completely. Secure with a wooden toothpick. Alternatively, place a strip of filling along the center of a leaf, roll it up, and secure both ends with toothpicks.

Steam the bundles over boiling water for 15 to 20 minutes, depending on their size. Serve immediately, piping hot, accompanied by chili sauce and extra Indonesian soy sauce.

SOUR SOUP WITH MEATBALLS

Here is a surprising but delicious combination: a light, piquant soup with robust meatballs and rice vermicelli.

4 ounces ground beef	1 teaspoon coriander seeds, crushed
4 ounces ground pork	1 teaspoon black peppercorns, crushed
1 tablespoon soy sauce	3 1/2 ounces rice vermicelli noodles
Seeds from 1 star anise, crushed	Chopped fresh cilantro, to garnish

FOR THE STOCK

1 stalk lemongrass, lightly bruised	1-inch piece gingerroot, chopped
1 onion, quartered	2-inch piece galangal, chopped
2 tablespoons tamarind pulp (page 5)	4 1/2 cups cold water
2 dried red chilies, chopped	

Mix together the ground beef and pork, soy sauce, star anise seeds, coriander seeds, and black peppercorns, and shape into small meatballs. Refrigerate for at least 20 minutes.

Meanwhile, put all the ingredients for the stock into a large saucepan, bring to a boil, and simmer for 10 minutes. Strain.

Return the stock to the saucepan and bring back to a slow boil. Add the chilled meatballs and simmer for 10 minutes or until the meatballs are cooked through. Add the rice vermicelli 2 or 3 minutes before the end of the cooking time. Serve hot, garnished with chopped cilantro.

MARINATED DUCK ON A BED OF NOODLES

This recipe demonstrates how plainly cooked noodles can be used as a foil for very rich ingredients.

3 tablespoons medium or sweet sherry	Salt and freshly ground black pepper
2 tablespoons sunflower oil	12 ounces duck breasts, skin removed
2 garlic cloves, crushed	7 ounces flat rice noodles
5 seeds from a star anise, crushed	Two 3-inch pieces cucumber, cut into
1 tablespoon soft dark brown sugar	matchsticks

Combine the sherry, 1 tablespoon of the oil, the garlic, star anise, brown sugar, and seasonings in a shallow dish. Add the duck breasts and turn them over so they are well coated. Leave the duck to marinate for at least 1 hour or, preferably, overnight.

Heat a heavy-bottomed skillet until it is very hot. Drain the duck breasts, reserving the marinade. Cook the duck in the hot pan over high heat for 6 to 8 minutes on each side. At the end of this time, add the reserved marinade, plus a little water if necessary, and simmer to make a sauce with a coating consistency. Remove the duck breasts and set aside to cool. Spoon the sauce into a small serving dish.

Cook the noodles in plenty of boiling water for 5 minutes or according to package directions. Drain and rinse under cold running water. Drain again and toss with the remaining oil and the cucumber matchsticks.

Divide the noodles between the serving plates. Slice the cooled duck thinly and arrange on top of the noodles. Serve with the sauce.

THAI EGG ROLLS

Thai egg rolls are more subtle in flavor than the perhaps more-familiar Chinese version. The filling in this recipe does not contain any meat, but you can add cooked ground chicken or pork. These are ideal for parties, as they are two-bite size.

Makes 32 egg rolls

2 tablespoons all-purpose flour	1 celery stick, finely chopped
2/3 cup water	2 scallions, finely chopped
2 1/2 ounces rice vermicelli noodles	1 1/2 cups finely chopped button mushrooms
1 tablespoon vegetable oil, plus more for deep-frying	2 teaspoons Indonesian soy sauce (kecap manis)
1 garlic clove, crushed	8 wonton wrappers, each 10 inches square
1 green bell pepper, finely chopped	

FOR THE DIPPING SAUCE

4 tablespoons rice vinegar	1/2 teaspoon salt
4 tablespoons sugar	1 small fresh red chili, finely chopped

Mix the flour and water together in a small pan over low heat, stirring constantly until the mixture is thick and translucent. Pour into a small bowl and set aside.

Blanch the rice vermicelli in boiling water for 30 seconds, then drain well. Snip into 1-inch pieces and set aside in a large bowl.

Heat 1 tablespoon of the oil in a wok or large, heavy-bottomed skillet over high heat. Add the garlic, green pepper, celery, scallions, and button mushrooms and stir-fry until the vegetables are soft. Add the Indonesian soy sauce. Use a slotted spoon to lift out the vegetables, then stir them into the rice vermicelli.

Divide each wonton wrapper into four squares. Place 2 teaspoons of the filling in the middle of each square. Fold three corners in and roll up to the fourth corner. Seal with a little of the flour and water paste.

To make the sauce, boil all the ingredients together, stirring constantly, until the sauce thickens, about 5 minutes. Leave to cool.

When you are ready to serve the egg rolls, heat oil in a wok or deep-fat fryer until a light haze appears—about 350°F/180°C. Deep-fry the egg rolls in batches until they are golden brown all over. Drain on plenty of paper towels to ensure a crisp finish. Serve immediately, accompanied by the sauce.

FRAGRANT CHICKEN BROTH

A good, filling broth. It is cheap to make, but sophisticated enough to serve to guests for a light lunch or after-theater supper.

1 chicken, weighing about 3 pounds	Juice of 1 lime
4 1/2 cups water	2 small fresh red chilies, seeded and sliced
2-inch piece gingerroot	3 tablespoons chopped fresh cilantro
2 onions, sliced	4 ounces flat rice noodles
Salt	2 scallions, thinly sliced
2 tablespoons bottled fish sauce	Shredded fresh red basil, to garnish
1 teaspoon black peppercorns	

Put the chicken in a large saucepan with the water, ginger, scallions, and a generous pinch of salt. Bring to a boil, then simmer for 45 minutes.

Lift out the chicken, and, when it is cool enough to handle, cut the meat from the bones. Slice the meat finely and set aside. Return the skin and bones to the saucepan. Add the fish sauce and peppercorns and simmer for 2 hours, skimming occasionally. Strain the stock and add the lime juice, chilies, and cilantro. Keep warm.

Cook the noodles in boiling water for 5 minutes or according to the package directions. Drain and divide between the serving bowls. Top with the sliced chicken and scallions and ladle in the hot soup. Garnish with shredded basil, and serve immediately.

NABEYAKI UDON

This dish is unusual because of the eggs cooked in the broth.

1 cup sliced shiitake mushrooms, or	8 thin slices kamaboko fishcake
1 ounce dried Chinese mushrooms	4 eggs
1 sheet konbu	1 scallion, finely chopped
Generous 6 cups water	
1 tablespoon miso paste	TO SERVE
14 ounces udon noodles	Dried bonito flakes
1 cup cubed firm tofu	Chili oil
3 ounces French-style green beans	Soy sauce

If using dried mushrooms, soak them in warm water for 15 minutes; drain and remove the stems. Meanwhile, soak the konbu in warm water for 15 minutes; drain, and cut into strips.

Put the water and miso paste into a large saucepan—at least a 12-cup capacity—and bring to a boil. Add the noodles and return to a slow boil, then add the tofu cubes, beans, mushrooms, konbu, and fishcake. Cover and simmer very gently for 5 minutes.

Carefully break the eggs into the simmering liquid, cover the pan, and cook for 4 to 5 minutes longer.

Ladle into serving bowls and garnish with the scallion. Serve immediately, accompanied by dried bonito flakes, chili oil, and soy sauce, so each person can flavor his dish according to taste.

CHICKEN VERMICELLI SOUP

This really is a meal in itself—nutritious and full of flavor.

1 chicken, weighing about 3 pounds	Salt and freshly ground black pepper
1 onion, quartered	2 quarts water
1 carrot, roughly chopped	3 ounces egg thread noodles
1 leek, roughly chopped	1 tablespoon butter
2 celery sticks, roughly chopped	1 tablespoon chopped fresh tarragon
1 teaspoon black peppercorns	
1 bouquet garni (fresh bay, parsley,	TO GARNISH
and thyme tied together in a bunch	2 tablespoons snipped fresh chives
with string)	Cayenne pepper

Cut the chicken breasts and legs from the body. Remove all the meat from the legs, as neatly as you can, and reserve the leg bones. Cut the chicken breast and leg meat into strips and set aside.

Preheat the oven to 400°C/200°F. Put the chicken carcass and leg bones in a roasting pan and roast for 45 minutes.

Transfer all the chicken bones and any cooking juices to a large saucepan or stockpot. Add the onion, carrot, leek, celery, peppercorns, bouquet garni, and a little salt. Pour in the water, bring to a boil, and simmer for 1 hour. Strain the stock, taste, and adjust the seasoning.

Break the noodles into small pieces (it is easiest to do this while they are still in the package).

Melt the butter in a large saucepan. Add the chicken strips and stir until cooked through. Season well. Add the stock, the noodles, and the tarragon. Simmer for 5 minutes, then serve hot, garnished with chives and cayenne pepper.

MUSHROOM AND GINGER BROTH

Look in gourmet food stores for mushroom ketchup, a condiment that adds an intense mushroom flavor. Not as common as tomato ketchup, mushroom ketchup was an early method for preserving the funghi.

1/2 ounce dried Chinese mushrooms	3 cups hot vegetable stock
4 ounces medium egg noodles	1 teaspoon mushroom ketchup (see above)
1 tablespoon sunflower oil	1 teaspoon light soy sauce
2 garlic cloves, crushed	Fresh cilantro leaves, to garnish
1-inch piece gingerroot, finely shredded	

Soak the Chinese mushrooms in 1 1/4 cups hot water for 30 minutes. Drain, reserving the soaking water. Remove and discard the stems, then slice the mushrom caps.

Soak the noodles in very hot water for 10 minutes.

Meanwhile, heat the oil in a wok or large skillet over high heat. Add the garlic, ginger, and sliced mushrooms and stir-fry for 2 minutes. Add the vegetable stock with the reserved mushroom soaking water and bring to a boil. Stir in the mushroom ketchup and soy sauce.

Drain the noodles and divide between the serving bowls. Ladle in the hot soup and serve immediately, garnished with cilantro leaves.

NOODLE-STUFFED ARTICHOKES

Make this in the spring when artichokes are cheap and abundant.

4 large globe artichokes
Juice of 1 lemon
3¹/₂ ounces soba noodles
1 cup shelled fresh or frozen peas
1 shallot, finely chopped

¹/₂ cup light cream
Salt and freshly ground black pepper
4 quail eggs
Cayenne pepper, to garnish

Snap the stem off each artichoke, pulling any tough stem fibers away with it. Trim off any tough outer leaves. Cut straight across the top, about one-third of the way down, so the hairy choke is exposed. Use scissors to cut the tough points off the remaining outer leaves. Trim the bottom so it is flat. As each artichoke is prepared, drop it into a large bowl of water to which you have added the lemon juice. Cook the artichokes in boiling salted water for 15 minutes.

Meanwhile, cook the noodles in boiling water for 4 minutes or according to the package directions. Drain and set aside.

Preheat the oven to 350°F/180°C. When the artichokes are tender, remove them from the pan and drain upside down on paper towels. As soon as they are cool enough to handle, use a teaspoon to scoop out the chokes.

Divide the noodles between the artichokes, piling them in the hollowed-out middles. Top with the peas and shallot. Arrange the artichokes in a baking pan.

Season the cream well with salt and pepper. Pour the cream into the artichokes, nearly to the top. Break a quail egg into the top of each one and sprinkle generously with cayenne pepper. Cover lightly with foil. Cook in the oven for 15 minutes. Serve piping hot.

NOODLE CRAB CAKES

These crab cakes are most delicious made with fresh white crabmeat. However, you can substitute frozen crabmeat, or a mixture of brown and white meat if fresh isn't available. This dish looks very pretty served with the chili sauce.

Makes 8 crab cakes

4 ounces rice vermicelli noodles
Vegetable oil for brushing
8 large fresh basil leaves
1 pound crabmeat, preferably fresh
5 tablespoons coconut milk
2 tablespoons red curry paste
2 eggs, lightly beaten

1 tablespoon bottled fish sauce
1 tablespoon chopped fresh cilantro
Salt and freshly ground black pepper
2 teaspoons cayenne pepper
¹/₂ cup mayonnaise
1 fresh red chili, seeded and finely chopped

Preheat the oven to 400°F/200°C. Cook the rice vermicelli in plenty of boiling water for 3 minutes, then drain well.

Brush 8 cups on one or two muffin trays lightly with oil, and line each tin with a single basil leaf. Divide the rice vermicelli between the muffin cups and arrange into neat nests.

Put the crabmeat, coconut milk, red curry paste, eggs, fish sauce, and cilantro in a bowl and stir together. Season generously with salt and pepper. Spoon a little of the crab mixture into each noodle nest. Bake for 15 minutes or until the crab mixture has risen and set.

Meanwhile, combine the cayenne pepper, mayonnaise, and chili in a small bowl. Serve as a dip with the crab cakes.

YUNNAN NOODLE SOUP

For authenticity, serve this in soup cups with tight-fitting lids, which you can buy in Oriental grocery stores.

5 cups strong chicken stock
4 shiitake mushrooms, halved
3¹/₂ ounces rice vermicelli noodles
3 ounces ground chicken
2 scallions, finely chopped
2 teaspoons soy sauce

3 tablespoons sunflower or peanut oil
1 teaspoon sesame oil
2 teaspoons chili oil
2-inch piece gingerroot, grated
1 garlic clove, crushed
Scant 1 bunch (3¹/₂ oz) watercress, chopped

Bring the stock to a boil in a large saucepan. Add the mushrooms, noodles, chicken, scallions, and soy sauce. Return to a boil, then remove from the heat. Cover and let stand for 5 minutes.

Meanwhile, put all the oils in a small saucepan with the ginger and garlic, and heat through until sizzling.

Stir the watercress into the soup and ladle into warmed serving bowls. Pour a little of the hot oil into each bowl, distributing the garlic and ginger evenly.. Let stand for 3 minutes longer, then serve.

SALAD NOODLES

Noodles make an ideal base for salads, providing contrasting backgrounds for the crunchiness and vibrant flavors of fresh vegetables, fruit, and herbs, with piquant dressings. Noodles also add substance to salads, creating excellent lunch or light supper dishes. All recipes in this chapter serve 4 to 6 unless otherwise indicated.

RICE NOODLES WITH PEANUT SAUCE

This recipe contains a deliciously rich and spicy version of satay sauce to dress rice noodles. It goes well with most marinated chicken dishes.

1/2 teaspoon cumin seeds
1/2 teaspoon coriander seeds
2 garlic cloves, crushed
1 small onion, quartered
1/2 red bell pepper, roughly chopped
1 tablespoon lemon juice
1 teaspoon salt

1/2 fresh red chili, seeded and sliced
1/2 cup coconut milk
Generous 3/4 cup crunchy peanut butter
1 cup water
4 ounces rice thread noodles
1 tablespoon chopped fresh cilantro, to garnish

First, make the peanut sauce. Grind the cumin and coriander seeds in a spice mill or with a mortar and pestle. Stir in the garlic.

Switch on the food processor or blender and add the quartered onion through the feed tube, followed by the cumin mixture, the red pepper, lemon juice, salt, chili, coconut milk, and peanut butter.

When all the ingredients are fully combined, transfer to a saucepan and stir in the water. Bring to a boil, then simmer for 2 to 3 minutes or until the sauce has a thin coating consistency. Let cool. If the sauce thickens as it cools, thin it to the correct consistency with a little water.

Cook the noodles in plenty of boiling water according to the package directions. Drain and refresh under cold running water. Drain well again. Combine the noodles with the peanut sauce, transfer to a serving dish, and garnish with chopped cilantro.

PUMPKIN SALAD WITH NOODLES

Pumpkin is a versatile ingredient in salads, soups, and stews. Here its slightly sweet flavor blends well with cilantro and sesame seeds.

18 ounces pumpkin or butternut squash
8 ounces soba noodles
2 tablespoons sesame oil
4 tablespoons sunflower oil
2 teaspoons red wine vinegar

1 teaspoon cayenne pepper, plus extra
Sea salt and freshly ground black pepper
4 tablespoons chopped fresh cilantro
2 tablespoons sesame seeds, toasted

Preheat the oven to 350°F/180°C. Cut the pumpkin into 2 large pieces, or the butternut squash in half lengthwise, and discard the seeds and fibers. Wrap in foil and bake for 45 minutes or until a fork pierces the flesh easily. Leave to cool, then peel away the skin, Cut the flesh into 1-inch cubes.

Cook the noodles in plenty of boiling water for 4 minutes or according to the package directions. Drain and refresh under cold running water. Drain well.

Combine the sesame oil, sunflower oil, red wine vinegar, and cayenne pepper, and season to taste with salt and pepper. Toss the noodles with this dressing until they are evenly coated. Transfer to a serving dish and toss in the pumpkin cubes and cilantro. Sprinkle with the sesame seeds and a pinch of cayenne pepper.

MINT AND LIME NOODLE SALAD

A fresh-tasting salad with a lot of crunch from the apples, celery, and the white radish called daikon.

4 ounces beancurd noodles
2 tablespoons lime juice
Salt and freshly ground black pepper
2 sharp dessert apples, cored and chopped

2 celery sticks, sliced
3/4 cup chopped daikon
2 tablespoons chopped fresh mint
1 cup alfalfa sprouts, to garnish

Pour boiling water over the noodles and let stand for 3 minutes or according to the package directions. Drain well and set aside to cool.

Add the lime juice to the noodles and season well. Add the apples, celery, daikon, and mint and toss together. Transfer to a serving bowl and sprinkle with the alfalfa sprouts. Serve immediately.

Crunchy Green Salad

CRUNCHY GREEN SALAD

Often something fresh and crunchy is needed in an Oriental meal, and this subtle salad fits the bill perfectly. It is pleasant and refreshing if served between courses, while the main course is stir-fried.

Serves 6 to 8

4 ounces egg thread noodles	*1 cup zucchini thinly sliced on a slant*
2 tablespoons balsamic vinegar	*4 cups finely shredded Chinese leaves*
2 tablespoons olive oil	*1 cup small broccoli florets*
Salt and freshly ground black pepper	*³/4 cup cashews, toasted and roughly*
4 ounces asparagus	*chopped*

Pour boiling water over the noodles and let stand for 3 minutes or according to the package directions. Drain and refresh under cold running water. Drain well again.

Combine the balsamic vinegar and olive oil, season to taste, and toss with the noodles until they are evenly coated.

Blanch the asparagus in boiling water, refresh under cold running water, and drain well again. If the spears are large, cut them into pieces. Toss together the noodles, asparagus, zucchini, Chinese leaves, and broccoli. Garnish with the toasted cashews. Cover and chill until ready to serve. Serve chilled.

SPICY SALAD WITH GINGER AND CHILI

Soba noodles have a definite, rich flavor, and a firm texture that makes them especially suitable to use in a salad.

7 ounces soba noodles	*1 fresh red chili, finely chopped*
Generous 1 cup chopped white cabbage	*2 tablespoons chopped fresh cilantro*
1 teaspoon turmeric	*2 scallions, finely chopped*
1 garlic clove, crushed	*Salt*
1 teaspoon grated gingerroot	*Juice of 1 lime*
1 tablespoon shredded pickled ginger	*¹/2 teaspoon onion pepper*
2 tablespoons sunflower oil	

Cook the noodles in plenty of boiling water for 5 minutes or according to the package directions. Drain, refresh under cold running water, and drain well. Gently stir the chopped cabbage with the noodles.

Combine the turmeric, garlic, gingerroot, pickled ginger, oil, chili, cilantro, and scallions and season to taste with salt. Toss this mixture with the noodles until they are evenly coated. Add lime juice and onion pepper to taste and serve cold.

HERBED NOODLE SALAD

The zing that abundant fresh herbs give to a dish is quite different from the flavor given by a light sprinkling toward the end of cooking.

14 ounces flat rice noodles	*4 tablespoons chopped fresh basil*
2 tablespoons sunflower oil	*Salt and freshly ground black pepper*
1 red bell pepper, finely chopped	*1 fresh green chili, halved and seeded*
4 tablespoons chopped fresh cilantro	*1 garlic clove, halved*
4 tablespoons chopped fresh mint	*Juice of 1 lemon*

Break the noodles into pieces about 2 inches long (it is easiest to do this while they are still in the package). Cook them in boiling water for 3 minutes or according to the package directions. Drain, refresh under cold running water, and drain well again.

Gently mix the noodles with the oil, red pepper, and herbs. Season generously with salt and pepper.

Rub the inside of a serving bowl with the cut sides of the halved chili and garlic clove; discard the chili and garlic. Transfer the noodle salad to the serving bowl and sprinkle with the lemon juice

WHITE NOODLE–CUCUMBER SALAD

A light but tasty salad, this combines the rich flavor of sesame with the coolness of cucumber.

3¹/₂ cups peeled and thinly sliced cucumber
Salt and freshly ground black pepper
2¹/₂ ounces rice vermicelli noodles
2 tablespoons sesame oil
2 tablespoons rice vinegar
1 tablespoon light soy sauce
Juice of 1 lime
2 cups bean sprouts
2 tablespoons sesame seeds, toasted

Rinse the cucumber under cold running water, then mix with 4 teaspoons of salt. Let stand for 15 minutes, then rinse and drain well.

Meanwhile, pour boiling water over the noodles and leave to stand for 5 minutes or according to the package directions. Drain and refresh under cold running water. Drain well again.

Mix together the sesame oil, rice vinegar, soy sauce, and lime juice. Season to taste, then toss with the noodles.

Stir the cucumber and bean sprouts into the noodles. Serve sprinkled with the sesame seeds.

BEET AND RADICCHIO SALAD

Beets were brought to the East by Russian invaders, and the Chinese, with their love of pickled vegetables, were soon pickling them. In this salad, their flavor contrasts well with the sharpness of the radicchio.

5 ounces mie noodles
1 tablespoon light soy sauce
1 tablespoon finely shredded pickled ginger
Salt and freshly ground black pepper
2 tablespoons sunflower oil
1 radicchio, shredded
3 ounces pickled beets, rinsed and quartered
3 scallions, chopped
3 tablespoons chopped fresh red basil

Pour boiling water over the noodles and let stand for 2 minutes or according to the package directions. Rinse and drain well, trying to keep the noodles in the nest shapes. Toss the noodles gently with the soy sauce and pickled ginger, and season well.

Heat the oil in a skillet. Add the radicchio and cook over medium heat for 2 to 3 minutes to soften. Remove from the heat and stir in the beets. Leave to cool.

Arrange the noodle nests on a serving dish. Spoon the beets, radicchio, and scallions over the dressed noodle nests and sprinkle with the red basil.

ONION NOODLE SALAD

The sweet, yet piquant, flavor of cooked white onions and scallions perfectly complements egg thread noodles and mushrooms.

12 small white onions, peeled
4 tablespoons olive oil
2 tablespoons soy sauce
Salt and freshly ground black pepper
12 scallions, finely chopped
1 tablespoon red wine vinegar
4 ounces egg thread noodles
1 tablespoon chopped fresh cilantro
1¹/₂ cups finely chopped button mushrooms

Preheat the oven to 350°F/180°C. Put the whole white onions in a roasting pan and toss with 1 tablespoon each of olive oil and soy sauce. Season well. Cover and bake for 20 minutes, basting often. Stir in half of the scallions, baste well, and return to the oven to bake for 10 minutes longer.

Meanwhile, combine the remaining oil and soy sauce with the vinegar, and season the dressing well.

Pour boiling water over the noodles and let stand for 4 minutes or according to the package directions. Drain and refresh under cold running water. Drain well. Toss with the dressing.

Let the onions cool for 5 minutes, then stir them into the noodles. Stir in the remaining scallions, the cilantro, and mushrooms, and serve immediately.

Beet and Radicchio Salad

LEMON–PEPPER SALAD

When used as a major flavoring, pepper adds a surprising rich smokiness, and a tingle on the tongue. Measure the ingredients for the dressing quite carefully—success depends on the balance of flavors.

6 ounces flat rice noodles	2 tablespoons sunflower oil
Grated zest of 1 lemon	1 teaspoon honey
3 tablespoons lemon juice	Salt
1 teaspoon mixed peppercorns, crushed	3/4 cup sliced red radishes
2 teaspoons Japanese seven-pepper spice or lemon pepper	

Cook the noodles in plenty of boiling water for 5 minutes or according to the package directions. Refresh under cold running water and drain.

Combine the lemon zest and juice, peppercorns, pepper, oil, and honey. Season with salt to taste.

Toss the noodles with the lemon dressing until they are evenly coated. Fold in the sliced radishes, and serve chilled.

CRISPY NOODLE SALAD

A fresh, colorful salad with crunch, this is ideal for a summer buffet, or as an accompaniment to an Oriental curry or a stir-fried dish.

2 ounces rice vermicelli noodles	1 orange bell pepper, finely chopped
3/4 cup butter	1 1/2 cups halved button mushrooms
2 tablespoons sesame seeds, toasted	2 scallions, finely chopped
2 tablespoons sunflower seeds, toasted	Sea salt and freshly ground black pepper
2 tablespoons pumpkin seeds, toasted	Shredded pickled ginger, to garnish
1 1/4 cups finely shredded red cabbage	

Crush the rice vermicelli into small pieces (it is easiest to do while it is still in the package, or in a plastic bag).

Melt the butter in a small saucepan and leave to cool slightly. As it cools you will notice the solids drop to the bottom of the pan. Pour off the clear butter at the top—this is clarified butter—and discard the solids.

Heat the clarified butter in a skillet and fry the crushed noodles in batches, stirring constantly and gently. Drain the fried noodles on paper towels. Mix with the toasted seeds.

Combine the cabbage, orange pepper, mushrooms, and scallions in a salad bowl, and season with a little salt and pepper.

Just before serving, add the crisp noodles and toasted seeds to the vegetables, and stir gently to mix. Serve immediately, before the noodles lose their crispness, garnished with a little pile of pickled ginger in the middle of the colorful salad.

JAPANESE UDON SALAD

Robust udon noodles are very satisfying in a salad. Fresh udon give a better result than dried ones because they are firmer and do not absorb as much dressing.

3/4 cup finely sliced cucumber	4 tablespoons shredded pickled ginger,
2 tablespoons salt	1 1/2 cups shredded Chinese leaves
8 ounces udon noodles	2 teaspoons Japanese seven-pepper spice or
2 teaspoons sunflower oil	lemon pepper

Put the cucumber into a colander, sprinkle with the salt, and let drain for 30 minutes. Rinse well under cold running water, then pat dry with paper towels.

Cook the noodles in plenty of boiling water for 2 minutes or according to the package directions. Drain well and toss with the oil.

Stir the cucumber and pickled ginger into the noodles, then add the Chinese leaves. Transfer to a serving bowl and sprinkle with the spice or lemon pepper.

RICE NOODLE SALAD

Here is a great salad for lunch or supper: crunchy vegetables and rice noodles in a dressing flavored with lemon and ginger. You can substitute or add other vegetables, according to what is available.

Serves 6–8

2 tablespoons lemon juice	7 ounces flat rice noodles
1 teaspoon mustard	2 cups bean sprouts
1 tablespoon grated gingerroot	1 carrot, cut into matchsticks
3 tablespoons sunflower oil	1 cup halved button mushrooms
Salt and freshly ground black pepper	7 ounces canned water chestnuts, sliced

Put the lemon juice, mustard, ginger, and oil into a bowl and whisk together. Season to taste with salt and pepper. Set aside.

Cook the noodles in plenty of boiling water according to the package directions. Drain well and snip them into small pieces, then toss with the dressing.

Put all the vegetables into a serving bowl and add the noodles. Toss to mix the vegetables evenly with the noodles, and serve.

Seafood Salad

Make this main-dish salad in the summer when palates need to be tempted with something cool and spicy. A generous bowl of garlic mayonnaise is the perfect partner.

8 squid, cleaned with tentacles discarded
2 tablespoons mirin
2 tablespoons rice vinegar
4 tablespoons sunflower oil
1 or 2 fresh red chilies, seeded and chopped
6 ounces medium egg noodles, broken into pieces
8 raw jumbo shrimp, shelled
1 red bell pepper, chopped
2 cups bean sprouts
4 scallions, sliced
6 ounces crabmeat, preferably fresh
1 tablespoon turmeric
2 garlic cloves, crushed
2 teaspoons ground coriander
1 tablespoon lemon juice
Salt

Cut the tapered end off each squid tube, and cut open down one side. Open out flat to form a square. Using a sharp knife, score a crisscross pattern on the inside of the squid. Put into a bowl with the mirin, vinegar, half of the oil, and the chilies. Leave to marinate for 1 hour.

Cook the egg noodles in boiling water for 5 minutes or according to the package directions. Drain and refresh under cold water. Drain well.

Pour the squid and its marinade into a saucepan and add the shrimp. Bring to a boil and simmer until tender (take care not to overcook). Drain and leave to cool.

Combine the red pepper, bean sprouts, scallions, and noodles in a bowl. Add the squid, shrimp, and crabmeat.

Mix together the remaining oil with the turmeric, garlic, and coriander, and stir into the salad. Season to taste with lemon juice and salt. Transfer to a serving bowl, cover and refrigerate until ready to serve. Serve chilled.

Malaysian Coconut Salad

Coconut milk is used extensively in Malaysian cooking, to give richness and enhance spices. Here, coconut flakes are added for extra texture.

8 ounces beancurd noodles
1 tablespoon lime juice
1 teaspoon sesame oil
1/2 cup coconut milk
Pinch of sugar
Pinch of salt
1 fresh red chili, seeded and chopped
1 stalk lemongrass, lightly bruised
1 teaspoon turmeric

1/4 cup natural peanuts, roasted and chopped
6 baby corn ears, halved lengthwise
2 cups bean sprouts

TO GARNISH
4 tablespoons coconut flakes
Lime slices

Pour boiling water over the noodles and let stand for 3 minutes or according to the package directions. Drain, rinse in cold water, and drain well again.

Combine the lime juice, sesame oil, coconut milk, sugar, salt, and red chili. Toss the noodles in this dressing.

Rub the lemongrass and turmeric around the inside of a serving bowl; discard the lemongrass. Toss the peanuts, baby corns, and bean sprouts with the noodles. Transfer to the serving bowl and garnish with the coconut flakes and lime slices.

Aromatic Noodle Salad

This is a delicately flavored salad, ideal as an accompaniment to richer dishes. Satsumas are a Japanese easy-peel fruit, similar to tangerines, or mandarin oranges.

8 ounces soba noodles
1 tablespoon sunflower oil
4 teaspoons Sichuan peppercorns
1 teaspoon black peppercorns
2 teaspoons star anise seeds, crushed
2 cups bean sprouts
1 can (15 oz) lychees, drained and halved

1 star fruit, thinly sliced
1 teaspoon soy sauce
2 tablespoons chopped fresh chervil
1 tablespoon lemon juice
Satsuma or tangerine slices, to garnish

Cook the noodles in boiling water for 4 minutes or according to the package directions. Drain, rinse under cold running water, and drain well again. Toss with the oil until the noodles are evenly coated.

Crush the Sichuan peppercorns and black peppercorns together. Combine these with the crushed star anise. Stir this spice mix through the noodles until it is evenly distributed. Gently toss in the bean sprouts, lychees, and starfruit. Sprinkle with the soy sauce, chervil, and lemon juice and toss lightly. Cover and chill until ready to serve. Serve chilled, garnished with satsuma or tangerine slices.

POULTRY

Versatile and popular, chicken is quick to cook and makes a satisfying midweek meal when it is combined with noodles and intriguing Oriental flavors. With rich sauces and other poultry, such as duck and quail, noodles are the ideal accompaniment. All the recipes in this chapter serve 4 to 6 unless otherwise indicated.

CHICKEN CUPS

These are delicious served with bottled sweet chili sauce that you can buy in supermarkets, as well as Oriental grocery stores. The noodle cups can be prepared in advance and cooked just before serving.

8 ounces medium egg noodles	1 egg, lightly beaten
12 ounces ground chicken	2 tablespoons sesame seeds, toasted
1/2 stalk lemongrass, finely chopped	1 teaspoon soy sauce
1 fresh green chili, seeded and finely chopped	2 tablespoons chopped fresh cilantro
	1-inch piece gingerroot, grated
1 cup coconut milk	8 large fresh basil leaves

Preheat the oven to 350°F/180°C. Cook the noodles in plenty of boiling water for 5 minutes or according to the package directions. Rinse and drain well.

Combine the chicken with the lemongrass, chili, coconut milk, egg, sesame seeds, soy sauce, chopped cilantro, and ginger in a large bowl.

Line the bottom of 8 cups of one or two muffin trays with a basil leaf. Spoon the noodles around the sides. Spoon in the chicken mixture. Bake for 15 minutes or until the chicken is cooked through.

SESAME–CHICKEN NOODLES

Sesame and chicken is a simple but delicious flavor combination.

8 ounces beancurd noodles	12 ounces boneless chicken, cut into strips
3 tablespoons sunflower oil	2 tablespoons sesame seeds, toasted
2 teaspoons sesame oil	
1 garlic clove, crushed	TO SERVE
4 cups shredded Chinese leaves	Shrimp crackers
3 scallions, sliced	Bottled chili sauce

Pour boiling water over the noodles and leave to stand for 3 to 5 minutes or according to the package directions. Drain well.

Heat the sunflower oil, sesame oil, and garlic in a wok or large skillet. When the mixture is hot, add the Chinese leaves and stir-fry for 2 minutes. Stir in the scallions, chicken, sesame seeds, and the noodles.

Stir-fry over high heat for about 3 minutes, using two spoons to lift and stir the mixture, so any excess liquid evaporates and the noodles do not become soggy. When the chicken is cooked through and the noodles are hot, serve immediately, accompanied by shrimp crackers and chili sauce.

CHICKEN IN THE BASKET

Deep-fried noodles are used as a basket in which to serve stir-fried chicken. To make the noodle baskets, you will need a cup-shaped wire draining spoon, which can be bought in Oriental grocery stores.

4 ounces rice vermicelli noodles	1 teaspoon soft light brown sugar
1 pound boneless chicken thighs, sliced	1 tablespoon fish sauce
1 garlic clove, crushed	2 tablespoons red curry paste
1-inch piece gingerroot, grated	Scant 1 cup coconut milk
Vegetable oil for deep-frying	About 2 tablespoons bottled oyster sauce
1 teaspoon sesame oil	Red bell pepper, finely sliced, to garnish
3 scallions, finely sliced	

Cover the noodles with boiling water and leave to stand for 1 minute, then drain well; remove as much moisture as possible because any left will make the hot frying oil spit.

Toss the chicken with the garlic and ginger; set aside while you prepare the deep-fried noodle baskets.

Heat oil in a wok or deep-fat fryer. Test the temperature with a piece of rice noodle: if it immediately rises to the surface and expands, the oil is ready; if not, wait a few moments and test again. Once the oil is hot, arrange one-sixth of the noodles in the wire draining spoon, pushing them against the sides and making a hollow in the middle. Immerse the spoon in the hot oil and fry for 10 seconds or until the shape of the noodle basket is set. Slip the basket off the spoon and turn it over in the oil. Cook for a little longer or until the basket is golden brown all over. Drain on plenty of paper towels, and keep warm. Shape and fry the remaining noodle baskets.

Pour off all but 1 tablespoon of the oil from the wok. Add the sesame oil and when it is hot, add the chicken and scallions and stir-fry over high heat for 2 minutes. Then add the sugar, fish sauce, curry paste, and coconut milk. Stir-fry for 1 minute longer or until the sauce begins to thicken. Add oyster sauce to taste.

Divide the chicken mixture between the deep-fried noodle baskets and serve garnished with strips of red pepper.

NOODLES WITH CHICKEN LIVERS

This is a filling meal in itself. It is cheap to make and very tasty!

6 ounces medium egg noodles	1 1/2 cups sliced shiitake mushrooms
1 tablespoon sunflower oil	2 tablespoons light soy sauce
2 garlic cloves, crushed	4 tablespoons dry sherry
2-inch piece gingerroot, grated	2 scallions, finely chopped,
6 ounces chicken livers, coarsely chopped	to garnish

Cook the noodles in boiling water for 5 minutes or according to the package directions. Drain, rinse, and drain again.

Heat the oil in a wok or large skillet. When hot, add the garlic, ginger, and chicken livers. Stir-fry just long enough to seal the livers. Add the mushrooms and noodles and stir-fry over high heat for 2 to 3 minutes or until the noodles are hot. Add the soy sauce and sherry and stir-fry for 2 minutes longer. Serve immediately, garnished with scallions.

ASSAM DUCK

An assam sauce is a sour tamarind sauce, traditionally used for laksa sour, which is a Malaysian fish dish. Here the sauce is served with a rich meat instead, complementing it perfectly.

4 duck breasts	3 tablespoons ground blanched almonds
Salt	3 tablespoons tamarind juice (page 5)
3 tablespoons shredded coconut	Pinch of sugar
4 shallots, chopped	14 ounces flat rice noodles
2 garlic cloves, chopped	1 3/4 cups bean sprouts
2-inch piece galangal, chopped	
1/2 teaspoon coriander seeds	TO GARNISH
3 fresh red chilies, seeded and chopped	2 tablespoons chopped fresh mint
5 tablespoons sunflower oil	1 scallion, finely sliced
1 teaspoon turmeric	1 stalk lemongrass, finely sliced

Rub salt into the duck breasts, and set aside for 20 minutes. Then cut into slices or large cubes.

Pound the coconut in a mortar and pestle until it releases a little oil and forms a thin paste. Add the shallots, garlic, galangal, coriander seeds, and red chilies and pound to a rough paste. (If preferred, transfer the pounded coconut to a spice grinder to make the paste.)

Heat the oil in a wok or large skillet. Add the duck and stir-fry over high heat for 2 minutes or until just cooked through but still pink in the middle. Drain the duck on plenty of paper towels.

Pour off all but 2 tablespoons of the oil from the wok. Add the spice paste, turmeric, almonds, tamarind, and sugar. Stir-fry over medium heat for 3 minutes. Return the duck to the pan and stir-fry for 2 minutes longer.

Meanwhile, cook the noodles in plenty of boiling water for 3 minutes or according to the package directions. Drain and transfer to warmed serving dishes. Top the noodles with the bean sprouts, then spoon the duck in its sauce on top. Garnish with the mint, scallion, and lemongrass, and serve immediately.

PEKING CHICKEN ON CRISPY RICE NOODLES

The unique flavors and textures of Peking duck are borrowed for this noodle dish, with chicken replacing the duck.

4 ounces rice thread noodles	2 tablespoons sugar
Vegetable oil for deep-frying	3 tablespoons water
1 teaspoon sesame oil	1 cucumber, finely shredded
1 pound boneless chicken, cut into strips	6 scallions, finely shredded
4 tablespoons bottled yellow bean sauce	6 radishes, shredded

Break the rice noodles into pieces while they are still in the package.

Heat oil in a wok to about 350°F/180°C. Stir the oil and drop in a few rice noodles. They should immediately rise to the surface; if they do not, the oil is not hot enough, so remove them with a slotted spoon, wait a few moments, and try again. Fry the noodles in batches until they are golden and crisp. Drain on paper towels. Repeat until all the noodles are fried, then keep them warm in a low oven.

Pour off all but 2 tablespoons of the oil from the wok. Add the sesame oil, then add the chicken and stir-fry for 3 minutes. Add the yellow bean sauce and stir-fry for 3 minutes longer. Add the sugar and water, then stir in the shredded cucumber and scallions and stir-fry for 3 minutes or until hot throughout.

Divide the noodles between the serving plates and spoon the chicken mixture over them. Sprinkle the radishes on top and serve.

TORI NANBA SOBA

A satisfying Japanese dish in which filling buckwheat noodles are topped with deep-fried chicken and served with a dipping sauce. The more buckwheat that soba noodles contain, the better they are (and the more expensive). Noodles with a buckwheat content of at least 40 percent are a good choice for this dish.

4 1/2 cups dashi broth or good, homemade chicken stock
14 ounces soba noodles
Vegetable oil for deep-frying
3 tablespoons all-purpose flour
10 ounces boneless chicken, cut into
3/8 x 1 1/2-inch strips

FOR THE BATTER
1 egg yolk
Scant 2 cups ice-cold water
Pinch of baking soda
1 teaspoon cayenne pepper
1 1/2 cups all-purpose flour

FOR THE DIPPING SAUCE
3 tablespoons mirin
3 tablespoons Japanese soy sauce
2 tablespoons dried bonito flakes
1 teaspoon miso paste
Salt
2/3 cup hot water

TO GARNISH
2 scallions, finely sliced
1 sheet nori, flaked

First, make the dipping sauce. Put the mirin in a small saucepan, bring to a boil, and boil to reduce by half. Stir in the soy sauce, bonito flakes, miso, a pinch of salt, and the hot water. Transfer to a serving bowl and set aside.

To make the batter, stir together the egg yolk, cold water, baking soda, and cayenne pepper in a large bowl. Sift in the flour and beat for 1 minute or until the batter is smooth; it should run off the spoon fairly easily, and be thinner than a traditional Western frying batter.

Bring the dashi broth or stock to a boil. Add the noodles and cook for 3 minutes. Drain the noodles, reserving the broth. Keep both noodles and broth warm.

Heat the oil in a wok or large skillet to about 350°F/180°C. Season the flour and lightly coat the chicken strips. Working in small batches, dip the chicken strips quickly into the batter and then immediately deep-fry in the hot oil until golden. Drain on plenty of paper towels.

Spoon the noodles into serving bowls and ladle in a little of the reserved broth. Top with the deep-fried chicken, and garnish with the scallions and flakes of nori. Serve immediately, accompanied by the dipping sauce.

CHILI RAMEN

This is a real winter warmer—low in fat and calories, but high in taste! Ramen noodle dishes are served in noodle bars all over Japan as a light one-pot meal. The noodles are slurped up into the mouth (the accepted way to eat them), as apparently this oxygenates the flavors. Once the noodles are eaten, the broth is drunk from the bowl.

2 teaspoons grated gingerroot
2 tablespoons bottled sweet chili sauce
10 ounces boneless chicken, cut into strips
14 ounces ramen noodles
1 teaspoon sesame oil
2 teaspoons sunflower oil
4 1/2 cups good chicken stock, or dashi broth, warmed

1 red bell pepper, finely chopped
1 fresh green chili, sliced
2 scallions, finely sliced

TO SERVE
Soy sauce
Dried bonito flakes
Chili oil

Combine the grated ginger and sweet chili sauce. Toss the chicken strips in this mixture until all pieces are evenly coated.

Cook the noodles in plenty of boiling water for 2 minutes or according to the package directions. Drain and keep warm.

Heat the sesame oil and sunflower oil in a wok or large skillet. When it is very hot, add the chicken and stir-fry for 2 to 3 minutes.

Pile the ramen noodles in serving bowls and ladle in the warm stock. Add the contents of the wok, the red pepper, green chili, and scallions. Serve immediately, accompanied by soy sauce, bonito flakes, and chili oil, for each person to add to taste.

WHITE MOUNTAIN

Pale ingredients are piled up into a peak to give an attractive presentation. Chinese pancakes are sold in Oriental grocery stores, and can also be bought in some Western supermarkets.

4 ounces flat rice noodles
2 boneless chicken breast halves, diced
1 cup diced firm tofu
1 red bell pepper, finely sliced
1 teaspoon salt
1 tablespoon cornstarch
2 tablespoons mirin or sake
1 egg white

8 Chinese pancakes
1 tablespoon sunflower oil
1-inch piece gingerroot, grated
1 garlic clove, crushed
Pinch of sugar
1 tablespoon light soy sauce
1 tablespoon rice vinegar
2 scallions, white part only, finely sliced

Pour boiling water over the noodles and let stand for 5 minutes. Drain well and keep warm.

Toss the chicken, tofu, and red pepper together with the salt, cornstarch, mirin or sake, and egg white in a small bowl. Set aside.

Heat the pancakes in a microwave or, covered with foil, in the oven.

Heat the oil in a wok or large skillet. Add the ginger and garlic, and stir. Add the chicken and red pepper mixture and stir-fry for 3 minutes over high heat. Add the sugar, soy sauce, and vinegar and stir-fry for 1 minute or until hot through.

Place a pancake on each plate and top with some noodles. Spoon the chicken mixture on top. Serve garnished with the chopped scallion.

CHICKEN NOODLE NESTS

Fried noodles, packed in long-life containers, are available in Oriental grocery stores, but they cannot compare to freshly made, and would not be suitable for this recipe.

Makes 4 nests

4 ounces flat rice noodles	1 teaspoon salt
2 cups dried instant mashed potatoes, reconstituted	1 pound boneless chicken, cut into 3/8 x 1 1/2-inch strips
1 teaspoon coriander seeds	1 garlic clove, crushed
1 teaspoon cumin seeds	1-inch piece gingerroot, grated
4 cloves	2 dried red chilies, seeded and sliced
1 whole star anise	4 scallions, sliced
1 teaspoon white peppercorns	1/2 cup coarsely chopped fresh cilantro
Vegetable oil for deep-frying	

Dip the rice noodles quickly into cold water, then drain and break into 2-inch pieces.

On the countertop or on a tray, space out 8 heaped teaspoons of the instant mashed potatoes, and press some noodles into each heap. Put another teaspoon of potatoes on top of each heap and press in some more noodles. Mold each mound roughly into 3-inch round nests; you may need to shape the nests in your hands.

Grind together the coriander seeds, cumin seeds, cloves, star anise, and peppercorns with a mortar and pestle or in a spice grinder. Set aside.

Heat 1 inch of oil in a wok or deep skillet. Test the temperature with a piece of noodle: if it does not immediately rise to the surface, the oil is not hot enough, so wait a minute and try again. When the oil is hot enough, drop in one nest and gently flatten it between two spoons to hold the shape. Fry, turning it over once, until it is golden brown. Remove and drain on plenty of kitchen paper. Fry the remaining nests, then season with salt and keep them warm in a low oven.

Pour off all but 2 tablespoons of the oil from the wok. Add the chicken, garlic, ginger, and chilies and stir-fry until the chicken is cooked through. Stir in the ground spices. Add the scallions and stir-fry for 2 minutes longer. Add the cilantro.

Put a deep-fried noodle nest on each plate and spoon some chicken on top. Top with another deep-fried nest and serve.

CHINESE QUAILS ON A BED OF NOODLES

Buy part-boned quails if you can find them—they are much easier to eat than quails that contain all their bones.

4 tablespoons honey	2 tablespoons sunflower oil
Seeds from 4 star anise, crushed	4 scallions, each cut into 3 pieces
1 teaspoon tamarind paste	2 celery sticks, cut into matchsticks
2 tablespoons soy sauce	2 carrots, cut into matchsticks, or
2 tablespoons dry sherry	8 baby carrots
2 tablespoons bottled yellow bean sauce	12 ounces Chinese flat wheat noodles
1 bay leaf	2 zucchini, cut into thin slices lengthways
4 garlic cloves, unpeeled and crushed lightly with the back of a knife	using a vegetable peeler
4 quails	3 tablespoons chopped fresh cilantro
	2 star fruit, sliced, to garnish

Combine the honey, crushed star anise seeds, tamarind, soy sauce, sherry, yellow bean sauce, and bay leaf, and set aside.

Put a garlic clove into the cavity of each quail. Heat the oil in a wok or large skillet. When it is hot, add the quails and fry over high heat until browned on all sides.

Add the honey paste and stir to coat the quails all over. Cover the wok and cook over high heat for 5 minutes. Remove the cover and cook for 5 minutes longer, turning the quails frequently and basting to glaze them. Add the scallions, celery, and carrots and cook, uncovered, for 5 minutes longer, stirring frequently.

Meanwhile, cook the noodles in plenty of boiling water for 4 minutes or according to the package directions. When the noodles are cooked, add the zucchini slices to the boiling water, then immediately drain the noodles and zucchini.

Serve the quails on a bed of the zucchini and noodles, with the vegetables arranged around them. Garnish the platter with the cilantro and star fruit.

STEAMED LETTUCE ROLLS

Do not worry if the lettuce rolls are not particularly neat before they go into the steamer, because they fuse together as they steam.

2 ounces beancurd noodles	1/2 cup finely diced firm tofu
6 ounces ground chicken	2 round lettuces
1/2 teaspoon white peppercorns, crushed	
4 teaspoons light soy sauce	TO SERVE
4 teaspoons grated gingerroot	Selection of pickled vegetables
31/2 ounces canned water chestnuts, drained and finely chopped	Soy sauce

Pour boiling water over the noodles and leave to stand for 3 to 5 minutes or according to the package directions. Drain and rinse, then drain again. Chop the noodles into 1-inch pieces and set aside.

Put the chicken into a bowl with the peppercorns, soy sauce, ginger, water chestnuts, and tofu. Mix well, then stir in the noodles.

Separate the lettuce leaves and rinse well. Remove the central stems. Gently pull out the edges of the leaves, so they lie flat. Spoon 1 tablespoon of the chicken mixture into the middle of each leaf and wrap up neatly. If the leaves are small, you may need to use two for each roll. Refrigerate until ready to cook.

Steam the rolls for 15 to 20 minutes or until the chicken is cooked through; they may need longer if the rolls have been refrigerated for a while. Serve hot, accompanied by pickled vegetables and soy sauce.

ICED LEMON CHICKEN

This is a delicious dish for parties, especially on a hot summer day.

3 lemons	2 tablespoons sunflower oil
3 thick slices gingerroot	2 teaspoons white wine vinegar
4 boneless chicken breast halves	2 teaspoons grated gingerroot
1 bay leaf	2 teaspoons light soy sauce
1 tablespoon Japanese seven-pepper spice or lemon pepper	1 teaspoon sugar
	2 scallions, finely chopped
6 ounces flat rice noodles	Salt and freshly ground black pepper
2 cups bean sprouts	Ice, to serve

Prick one of the lemons all over with a skewer, and put it into a large pan with the ginger slices, chicken breasts, bay leaf, and enough water to cover. Bring to a boil, then poach the chicken gently for about 15 minutes or until it is just cooked through.

Drain the chicken and leave to cool, then sprinkle with the pepper spice. Grate the zest of the remaining lemons over the chicken.

Cook the noodles in boiling water according to the package directions. Drain, rinse well, and drain again. Toss with the bean sprouts.

Squeeze 1 tablespoon juice from a lemon, and put into a bowl with the oil and vinegar. Add the grated ginger, soy sauce, sugar, and scallions. Whisk well to make a thick dressing. Taste and season.

Put a layer of ice in a serving bowl. Spoon in the noodles and bean sprouts. Slice each chicken piece into 6 pieces, and arrange on the noodles. Add the dressing and serve at once, before the ice melts.

SATAY CHICKEN WITH NOODLES

The chicken is marinated and cooked on wooden skewers—available from Oriental grocery stores—which must be soaked in water for 20 minutes before use.

11/2 pounds boneless chicken, cut into 3-inch strips	2 tablespoons soy sauce
1 small onion, sliced	2 tablespoons sunflower oil
2 garlic cloves, crushed	1 tablespoon lemon juice
1 teaspoon ground coriander	1 teaspoon soft dark brown sugar
1 teaspoon ground cumin	8 ounces egg thread noodles
2 fresh red chilies, seeded and roughly chopped	2 tablespoons chopped fresh cilantro
	2 tablespoons chopped fresh mint
1-inch piece gingerroot, grated	2 scallions, finely sliced

FOR THE PEANUT SAUCE

1 small onion, quartered	1 tablespoon lemon juice
2 garlic cloves, crushed	1 teaspoon salt
1 teaspoon coriander seeds	1/2 cup coconut milk
1 teaspoon cumin seeds	1 cup crunchy peanut butter
1/2 fresh red chili	1 cup water

Soak 12 wooden skewers in water for 20 minutes. Thread the chicken onto the soaked skewers.

Combine the onion, garlic, coriander, cumin, chilies, ginger, soy sauce, oil, lemon juice, and brown sugar in a shallow dish. Add the chicken skewers and refrigerate for 2 hours.

Meanwhile, make the peanut sauce. In a food processor, combine the onion quarters, garlic, spices, and chili. Add the remaining sauce ingredients, except the water, in the order listed, and process until well mixed. Transfer to a saucepan and blend in the water. Bring to a slow boil and simmer until thick. Pour into a serving bowl and set aside.

Preheat the broiler to medium-hot. Broil the chicken skewers for 10 minutes, turning and basting frequently.

Meanwhile, pour boiling water over the noodles and let stand for 3 minutes or according to the package directions. Drain and stir in the cilantro, mint, and scallions.

Serve the chicken satay sticks on a bed of noodles, accompanied by the peanut sauce.

Steamed Lettuce Rolls

CHILI CHICKEN WITH NOODLES

This recipe is full of flavor and easy to make—it's great for a midweek supper, served with a green salad.

8 ounces medium egg noodles	1/2 teaspoon freshly ground black pepper
1 tablespoon sunflower oil	12 ounces boneless chicken, either thigh
1 red bell pepper, finely diced	or breast, cut into 2-inch strips
6 scallions, finely sliced	Salt
1 teaspoon ground coriander	Juice of 2 limes
2 teaspoons red-pepper flakes or bottled	2 cups bean sprouts
chili sauce	

Cook the noodles in plenty of boiling water for 5 minutes or according to the package directions. Drain.

Heat the oil in a wok or large skillet. Add the red pepper and scallions and stir-fry over high heat for 1 minute. Add the ground coriander, red-pepper flakes or sauce, and black pepper.

Add the chicken and stir-fry until it is just cooked through and coated with the spice mixture. Add salt to taste and stir in the lime juice, bean sprouts, and noodles. Serve immediately.

CHICKEN RAMEN

If you are a noodle fanatic, you'll soon be hooked on ramen dishes because they can be altered so easily, according to the ingredients you have on hand and the flavorings you particularly like.

2/3 cup mirin	4 boneless chicken breast halves
2/3 cup soy sauce	2 ounces konbu
2/3 cup chicken stock	4 1/2 cups dashi broth
1 tablespoon sugar	14 ounces ramen noodles

TO SERVE

2 scallions, finely sliced	Grated gingerroot
Soy sauce	Chili oil

Put the mirin into a small saucepan, bring to a boil, and boil to reduce by half. Remove from the heat and stir in the soy sauce, chicken stock, and sugar. Pour into a shallow dish. Add the chicken and leave it to marinate in this mixture for 1 hour only.

Soak the konbu in warm water for 15 minutes; drain and slice finely.

Bring the dashi broth to a boil. Add the noodles and cook for 2 minutes. Drain, reserving the broth. Keep both noodles and broth hot.

Heat a wok or large open pan to searing temperature. Add the marinated chicken breasts and press down with a spatula. Cook for 5 minutes, turning them over once. This fast cooking over high heat keeps the chicken moist on the inside and retains maximum flavor.

Arrange the noodles in serving bowls and add a few pieces of soaked konbu. Pour the hot broth over the noodles. Slice the chicken breasts and arrange on top of the noodles. Serve immediately, accompanied by scallions, soy sauce, ginger, and chili oil, so each person can flavor his dish to taste.

RED CURRY WITH NOODLES

You can buy red curry paste in jars, but once you have tasted the freshly made version, there will be no going back! The paste keeps for up to three weeks in a sealed jar in the refrigerator. Alternatively, it can be frozen; be sure to wrap the portions tightly, otherwise the pungent flavor will permeate other foods in the freezer.

1 1/2 pounds boneless chicken thighs	4 ounces snow peas
or breast, cut into strips	8 ounces medium egg noodles
1 cup coconut milk	1 tablespoon chopped fresh cilantro
1/4 teaspoon soy sauce	10 fresh basil leaves, roughly chopped
1/2 cup baby corn, halved lengthwise	

FOR THE RED CURRY PASTE

6 fresh or dried red chilies, halved,	Grated zest of 1 lime
seeded, and blanched	4 garlic cloves, chopped
2 teaspoons cumin seeds	3 shallots, chopped
2 teaspoons coriander seeds	2 kaffir lime leaves, mid-rib removed and
1-inch piece galangal, chopped	leaves shredded
1/2 stalk lemongrass, chopped	1 tablespoon sunflower oil
1 teaspoon salt	

To make the curry paste, grind all the ingredients together using a large mortar and pestle, or in a food processor or a spice grinder.

Heat a wok or large, heavy-bottomed skillet over high heat and stir-fry 3 tablespoons of the red curry paste until fragrant. Add the chicken strips and stir-fry over high heat until they are sealed on all sides.

Add the coconut milk, soy sauce, baby corn, and snow peas. Bring to a slow boil and simmer for 10 minutes or until the vegetables are cooked but still crisp.

Meanwhile, cook the noodles in plenty of boiling water for 5 minutes or according to the package directions. Drain and keep warm.

Stir the cilantro and basil into the curry. Divide the noodles between the serving bowls and spoon the hot curry on top.

FISH & SHELLFISH

Seafood is a popular ingredient in Southeast Asia and throughout the Far East; fish and shellfish—particularly shrimp and squid—are frequently used in noodle dishes. Because the cooking times are usually very quick, the seafood retains its succulent texture and fresh flavor. All recipes in this chapter serve 4 to 6, unless otherwise indicated.

INDONESIAN STIR-FRIED NOODLES

This dish, called *mee goreng*, is eaten all over Indonesia, Singapore, and Malaysia, as is its rice equivalent, *nasi goreng*.

8 ounces egg thread noodles	*6 ounces shelled raw jumbo shrimp, or*
1 egg	*cooked shelled shrimp*
3 tablespoons water	*1 tablespoon Indonesian soy sauce*
2 tablespoons sunflower oil	*Salt*
4 shallots, sliced	*Fresh cilantro leaves, to garnish*
2 garlic cloves, crushed	
1 green bell pepper, finely chopped	*FOR THE ACCOMPANIMENTS*
1 red bell pepper, finely chopped	*1/2 cup thinly sliced cucumber*
1 teaspoon ground coriander	*Rice vinegar*
1 teaspoon ground cumin	*Sugar*
1 teaspoon grated gingerroot	*3 tablespoons chopped roasted peanuts*
3 fresh red chilies, sliced	*2 scallions, finely sliced*
1 teaspoon shrimp paste	*3 tomatoes, thinly sliced*
1 cup diced boneless chicken breast	*Shrimp crackers*
1 cup diced boneless pork	

Cook the noodles in plenty of boiling water for 3 minutes or according to the package directions. Drain, rinse well, and drain again.

Lightly beat the egg with the water. Put a few drops of the oil into a wok. When it is quite hot, make a very thin omelet with the egg mixture. Roll up the omelet and let cool. When completely cool, cut into thin strips.

To prepare the accompaniments, lightly pickle the cucumber in equal quantities of rice vinegar and sugar for 5 minutes, then drain. Put into a serving dish. Put the remaining accompaniments in individual dishes.

Heat the remaining oil in the wok. Add the shallots and garlic and stir-fry over high heat for 2 to 3 minutes or until soft. Add the green and red peppers and stir-fry for 1 minute, then add the ground coriander and cumin, ginger, chilies, and shrimp paste. Stir well. Add the chicken and pork. If using raw shrimp, add them at this stage; if using cooked shrimp, add at the end of cooking, with the noodles. Stir-fry until the chicken, pork, and shrimp are cooked.

Add the noodles and stir in, using two spoons to lift and stir until they are evenly coated with the sauce and heated through. Add the soy sauce and salt to taste. Scatter with some cilantro leaves and the omelet strips, and serve hot, with the accompaniments.

SALMON-COCONUT CURRY

A rich, mild curry for a special occasion. It is equally good with shrimp or any firm-fleshed fish, such as monkfish.

1 tablespoon sunflower oil	*1 1/4 pounds salmon, diced*
1 onion, chopped	*1/2 cup coconut milk*
1 garlic clove, chopped	*1 can (7 oz) crushed tomatoes*
1 fresh green chili, seeded and chopped	*Juice of 1 lemon*
1-inch piece gingerroot, chopped	*Salt and freshly ground black pepper*
1 teaspoon turmeric	*8 ounces rice thread noodles*
1 teaspoon paprika	*2 tablespoons chopped fresh cilantro*
Pinch of ground cumin	

Heat the oil in a wok or large skillet. Add the onion, garlic, chili, and ginger, then stir in the turmeric, paprika, and cumin. Cook over low heat for 2 minutes, stirring occasionally.

Increase the heat and add the salmon. Stir gently, until the salmon is coated in the spices and sealed on all sides. Add the coconut milk and tomatoes, and season to taste with lemon juice, salt, and pepper. Reduce the heat and leave to simmer for 2 to 3 minutes.

Meanwhile, cook the noodles in plenty of boiling water for 3 minutes or according to the package directions. Drain well.

Spoon the curry over the noodles and serve immediately, garnished with the chopped cilantro.

CANTONESE OYSTER NOODLES

A wide variety of fresh seafood is available in southern China, and is often eaten in simple dishes with egg noodles, such as this one. If fresh oysters are not available, substitute canned.

5 ounces egg thread noodles	24 fresh oysters, shelled
2 tablespoons sunflower oil	3 tablespoons dry sherry
4 scallions, finely sliced	1 tablespoon light soy sauce
2 garlic cloves, crushed	

Pour boiling water over the noodles to cover them and let stand for 3 minutes or according to the package directions. Drain, rinse, and drain again. Keep warm.

Heat the oil in a wok or large skillet and stir-fry the scallions and garlic over medium heat for 1 minute; do not let the garlic brown too much.

Add the oysters and sherry and stir-fry over high heat for 1 minute. Stir in the soy sauce. Spoon the oysters over the noodles and serve.

SWORDFISH WITH CUCUMBER AND NOODLE CUPS

Swordfish has a deliciously meaty texture. Choose large steaks for the best flavor and texture. The cucumber sauce also works well with quickly cooked beef, pork, trout, and shellfish.

2 tablespoons mirin or dry sherry	2 tablespoons chopped capers
1 tablespoon black peppercorns, crushed	2 tablespoons snipped fresh chives
1 tablespoon sunflower oil	1 teaspoon wine vinegar
4 swordfish steaks, each weighing about	3 tablespoons mayonnaise
6 ounces	1 tablespoon heavy cream
1/2 cucumber, diced	4 ounces rice thread noodles
1 tablespoon salt	

Combine the mirin, peppercorns, and oil. Put the swordfish in a nonmetallic dish and pour the oil mixture over. Turn the fish to coat evenly with the marinade. Cover and refrigerate for up to 8 hours.

Put the diced cucumber in a bowl with the salt, mix well, and leave for 20 minutes. Drain and rinse in a strainer. Put the cucumber in a bowl and add the capers, chives, and vinegar. Combine the mayonnaise and cream and stir into the cucumber mixture. Set aside.

Preheat the oven to 425°F/220°C. Wrap each piece of swordfish individually in foil and bake for 10 minutes.

Meanwhile, pour boiling water over the noodles to cover them and let stand for 3 to 5 minutes or according to the package directions. Drain well and keep warm.

Divide the noodles between the serving plates, making a compact pile on each. With the handle of a wooden spoon, or your thumb, make a deep indentation in each pile of noodles. Spoon the cucumber sauce into this indentation. Serve alongside the swordfish.

SHRIMP TEMPURA SOBA

Tempura batter is different from a Western fritter or frying batter in that it is very light and not particularly well blended. It should be used as soon as it is made.

Vegetable oil for deep-frying	1 tablespoon finely shredded nori
12–18 raw jumbo shrimp, shelled	1 tablespoon finely grated gingerroot
4 1/2 cups dashi broth	3 scallions, finely chopped
18 ounces soba noodles	

FOR THE DIPPING SAUCE

3 tablespoons mirin or dry sherry	3 tablespoons dried bonito flakes
3 tablespoons Japanese soy sauce	About 1 teaspoon wasabi paste
3/4 cup chicken stock	Pinch of salt

FOR THE BATTER

1 egg yolk	Pinch of baking soda
Scant 2 cups ice-cold water	1 1/2 cups all-purpose flour

First, make the dipping sauce. Put the mirin into a small saucepan, bring to a boil, and boil to reduce by half. Add the soy sauce, chicken stock, and bonito flakes, and bring back to a slow boil. Immediately remove from the heat and strain. Stir in the wasabi paste and salt to taste. Transfer to a serving bowl and set aside.

Heat oil in a wok or deep-fat fryer to about 350°F/180°C. To make the batter, combine the egg yolk and water in a bowl and beat well with a fork. Sift in the baking soda and flour. Beat well with a fork. Dip the shrimp into the batter and then immediately deep-fry them in the hot oil until puffed and golden. Drain on paper towels and keep warm.

Heat the dashi broth. Meanwhile, cook the noodles in boiling water for 4 minutes or according to the package directions. Drain.

Spoon the noodles into warmed serving bowls and ladle in the hot broth. Sprinkle with the shredded nori, ginger, and scallions. Top each bowl with 3 shrimp. Serve at once, with the dipping sauce.

CHILI–GARLIC SHRIMP

The rich combination of juicy shrimp, garlic, and chilies is a favorite with many people. Here it is served on a bed of rice noodles.

8 ounces flat rice noodles	Pinch of salt
4 tablespoons butter	Freshly ground black pepper
2 garlic cloves, crushed	10 ounces shelled raw jumbo shrimp
2 fresh red chilies, finely chopped	4 tablespoons chopped fresh cilantro

Pour boiling water over the noodles to cover and let stand for 5 minutes or according to the package directions. Drain and keep warm.

Melt the butter in a wok or large skillet. When it is foaming, add the garlic and chilies. Season and add the shrimp. Stir-fry over high heat for 2 minutes or until cooked.

Serve the shrimp on the noodles, sprinkled liberally with cilantro.

SAFFRON NOODLES WITH RED SNAPPER

This recipe comes from the Pacific Rim, where young cooks use seafood in the most wonderful and imaginative ways!

2 tablespoons extra virgin olive oil
3 tomatoes, chopped
3/4 cup pitted and roughly chopped black olives
1 tablespoon chopped capers
Salt and freshly ground black pepper
4–6 red snapper fillets, each weighing about 6 ounces

2 teaspoons packed saffron threads
1 tablespoon boiling water
8 ounces mie noodles
1 tablespoon chopped fresh flat-leaf parsley
1 tablespoon lemon juice

Preheat the oven to 350°F/180°C. Gently heat the olive oil in a saucepan, and stir in the tomatoes, olives, and capers. Season generously with salt and black pepper. Remove from the heat.

Arrange the fish fillets on a baking tray. Spoon the tomato mixture over, pressing it well into the flesh. Bake the fish for 10 minutes or until just cooked through.

Meanwhile, lightly crush the saffron threads, and leave to infuse in the boiling water.

Pour boiling water over the noodles and let stand according to the package directions. Drain well, keeping the nests together as much as possible. Toss the noodles gently with the saffron liquid to color them evenly. Season generously with black pepper.

Divide the saffron noodles between the serving plates, and place a fish fillet on each bed of noodles. Stir the parsley and lemon juice into the sauce left in the baking tray, taste, and adjust the seasoning. Spoon over the fish fillets.

SEAFOOD RAMEN

This is a deliciously filling Japanese noodle stew, in which the flavors are subtle but intense. Nori, a sea vegetable sold dried in very thin sheets, adds an unusual, bittersweet flavor.

6 1/4 cups fish stock
8–12 raw jumbo shrimp, shelled
4–6 scallops, shelled
12–18 baby squid, cleaned with tentacles discarded and bodies sliced
14 ounces ramen noodles
About 2 tablespoons soy sauce

4–6 thin slices Japanese fish cake—either kamaboko or naruto
1 sheet nori, flaked

TO SERVE
2 scallions, finely chopped
Grated gingerroot
Soy sauce

Heat the fish stock to boiling. Steam the shrimp, scallops, and squid over the stock for 4 minutes.

Meanwhile, cook the noodles in plenty of boiling water for 2 minutes or according to the package directions. Drain. Divide the noodles between the serving bowls.

Flavor the fish stock with soy sauce to taste and ladle it over the noodles. Arrange the shrimp, scallops, squid, and Japanese fish cake on top. Scatter with the nori flakes. Serve immediately, accompanied by the scallions, ginger, and soy sauce, to be added to taste.

SINGAPORE NOODLES

When eaten on the street in Singapore, these noodles come in many variations, depending on what the stallholder has available that day. Feel free to experiment with the ingredients here.

8 ounces rice thread noodles
2 tablespoons sunflower oil
2 shallots, sliced
2 garlic cloves, crushed
2 tablespoons grated gingerroot
1/2 red bell pepper, shredded
1/2 green bell pepper, shredded
1 teaspoon red-pepper flakes
1 tablespoon ground coriander

1 cup diced boneless pork
Generous 1 cup diced boneless chicken
6 ounces shelled raw shrimp, diced, or cooked shelled shrimp
1/3 cup thawed frozen peas
1 tablespoon soy sauce
Juice of 1 lemon
3 tablespoons chopped fresh cilantro

Pour boiling water over the noodles to cover them; let stand for 4 minutes or according to the package directions. Drain and set aside.

Heat the oil in a wok over high heat. Add the shallots, garlic, ginger, red pepper, green pepper, and pepper flakes. Stir-fry for 2 minutes or until the shallots are soft. Stir in the ground coriander, followed by the pork, chicken, and raw shrimp; if using cooked shrimp, add them at the end of cooking, with the noodles. Stir-fry over high heat for 4 minutes or until the chicken and pork are cooked through.

Add the noodles and peas to the wok and use two spoons to lift and stir until the noodles are coated evenly with the sauce and hot through. Add the soy sauce and lemon juice. Serve hot, garnished with the chopped cilantro.

SHELLFISH NOODLES

This dish looks very colorful, with the mussels, clams, and shrimp still in their shells. However, you will need to provide finger bowls and plenty of paper napkins.

3 pounds mixed shellfish, such as
live mussels and clams, raw jumbo
shrimp in their shells, and scallops,
preferably with their corals left on
2 tablespoons sunflower oil
2 scallions, finely chopped
1 tablespoon finely chopped gingerroot
1–2 fresh red chilies, finely chopped

1 garlic clove, crushed
1 teaspoon turmeric
4 tomatoes, skinned, seeded, and chopped
8 ounces rice vermicelli noodles
4 tablespoons chopped fresh mixed herbs,
such as chives, parsley, and chervil
Salt and freshly ground black pepper

Prepare the shellfish according to type: scrub the mussels and clam shells, scraping off any barnacles, and wash in several changes of fresh cold water; rinse the shrimp and scallops and pat dry.

Heat the oil in a wok or large skillet. Add the scallions, ginger, chilies, garlic, turmeric, and tomatoes and stir-fry over high heat for 2 minutes. Reduce the heat, add the shellfish, cover the wok, and cook for 5 minutes, stirring frequently.

Meanwhile, pour boiling water over the noodles to cover them; let stand for 4 minutes or according to the package directions. Drain well and toss with the herbs.

Discard any unopened shellfish, taste the sauce, and adjust the seasoning if necessary. Serve immediately on a bed of noodles.

SAFFRON SCALLOPS ON A BED OF NOODLES

This is a very pretty dish, with cream-colored scallops, red tomato, and green chives in a saffron-yellow sauce. It is best made with fresh scallops, rather than frozen.

1 teaspoon saffron threads, lightly crushed
2 tablespoons warm water
8 ounces medium egg noodles
4 tablespoons butter
16 large scallops, shelled

1 scallion, finely sliced
3 tomatoes, skinned, seeded, and chopped
3 tablespoons snipped fresh chives
Pinch of salt

Combine the saffron and warm water, and leave to infuse.

Cook the noodles in plenty of boiling water for 5 minutes or according to the package directions. Drain well and keep warm.

Melt the butter in a pan just large enough to hold all the scallops. Stir in the saffron liquid. When the butter is medium-hot, add the scallops, scallions, tomatoes, and chives. Cover and simmer for 7 minutes. Add salt. Spoon the scallops and sauce over the noodles. Serve.

ICED LOBSTER SALAD

A sophisticated Pacific Rim salad idea—the perfect way to prepare lobster in the summer. You can use two 1-pound lobsters if you prefer.

4 ounces rice vermicelli noodles
2-pound lobster, cooked
Sliced pickled ginger, finely chopped

Japanese seven-pepper spice or lemon pepper
2 tablespoons chopped fresh chervil
2 tablespoons chopped fresh red basil

Break the vermicelli into little pieces while it is in the package. Put it in a bowl, add boiling water to cover, and let stand for 3 minutes or according to package directions. Drain, rinse, and drain again.

Remove the legs from the lobster, close to the body. Snap each leg in half at the joint and remove the meat with a skewer. Break each claw off near the body, and crack the claw shell with a mallet. Remove the meat from each claw, in one piece if possible, including the meat from the pincers. Discard the blade that you will find in the claw meat.

Cut off the head, and lay the lobster on its back. Use a heavy knife or kitchen scissors to cut through the belly shell down the middle. Pull open the shell and remove the meat in one piece. Cut the meat across into 8 equal pieces.

Put a layer of ice in a serving dish and spoon the rice vermicelli over it. Sprinkle with some pickled ginger. Arrange the pieces of lobster, including the meat from the claws and legs, neatly over the top. Sprinkle with Japanese pepper, chervil, and red basil, and serve immediately, before the ice melts.

Saffron Noodles with Red Snapper

TERIYAKI SALMON WITH NOODLES

Bottled teriyaki marinade and sauce is sold in supermarkets, but a fuller flavor will be achieved by making your own.

6 tablespoons mirin or medium-dry sherry
6 tablespoons soy sauce
6 tablespoons chicken stock
4 salmon fillets, weighing about 6 ounces each

8 ounces medium egg noodles
2 tablespoons sesame oil
2 tablespoons finely snipped fresh chives
3 scallions, finely chopped

First, make the teriyaki sauce. Put the mirin or sherry in a saucepan, bring to a boil, and simmer for 2 minutes or until reduced by half. Stir in the soy sauce and stock. Remove from the heat.

Preheat the broiler to very hot, and line the broiler pan with foil. Arrange the salmon fillets in the pan and brush with the teriyaki sauce. Broil for 5 to 6 minutes on each side, basting often with the sauce.

Meanwhile, cook the noodles in plenty of boiling water for 5 minutes or according to the package directions. Drain and stir in the sesame oil, chives, and scallions.

Serve the salmon on a bed of piping hot noodles, accompanied by any remaining teriyaki sauce.

SPICY SHRIMP NOODLES

Fresh, tiny brown shrimp—also called popcorn shrimp—are ideal for this recipe. You can, however, also use ordinary shelled large shrimp.

2 ounces beancurd noodles
1 tablespoon sunflower oil
2 shallots, finely chopped
2 teaspoons ground coriander
1/2 teaspoon ground cumin
1/2 teaspoon black pepper

1 teaspoon turmeric
Pinch of salt
1 teaspoon red-pepper flakes
1 garlic clove, crushed
1 tablespoon lemon juice
8 ounces raw, shelled shrimp

Cover the noodles with boiling water and let stand for 3 minutes or according to the package directions. Drain and keep warm.

Heat the oil in a wok or large skillet. Add the shallots and cook over medium heat for 10 minutes, without browning. Add the coriander, cumin, pepper, turmeric, salt, red-pepper flakes, and the garlic. Squeeze the lemon juice over and stir in the shrimp.

As soon as the shrimp are cooked and the mixture is hot, toss with the noodles and serve immediately.

MALAYSIAN SWEET CURRY

Called *laksa lemak* in Malaysia, this is traditionally made just with fish, but chicken is also a good addition. The texture of this curry is very liquid—once the noodles have been slurped and the shrimp and chicken eaten, the coconut broth is sipped from the bowl.

1 chicken, weighing about 2 1/4 pounds
2 tablespoons sunflower oil
4 shallots, sliced
2 garlic cloves, crushed
2 fresh red chilies, very finely chopped
1 fresh green chili, seeded and chopped
1-inch piece gingerroot, grated
2 teaspoons ground coriander
1 stalk lemongrass, finely chopped
2 teaspoons turmeric
12 ounces raw jumbo shrimp in their shells
2 cups bean sprouts

4 ounces flat rice noodles
1 3/4 cups coconut milk
2 tablespoons finely chopped fresh cilantro, to garnish
Lime wedges, to serve

FOR THE STOCK
2 bay leaves
1 stalk lemongrass, crushed
3 kaffir lime leaves
6 black peppercorns
1 onion, halved

Put the chicken in a pan with enough water to cover and add the stock ingredients. Bring to a boil and simmer gently for about 1 hour or until the chicken is cooked through. Remove from the heat and leave to cool in the stock.

When the chicken is cool enough to handle, remove it from the pan and cut all the meat from the carcass; set the meat aside. Discard the skin and return the bones to the stock. Bring to a boil and boil to reduce to 4 1/2 cups. Strain the stock and set aside.

Heat the oil in a wok or large skillet. Add the shallots, garlic, red and green chilies, ginger, ground coriander, lemongrass, and turmeric. Stir-fry for 1 to 2 minutes or until the shallots are soft. Add the strained chicken stock and the shrimp and bring to a boil.

Meanwhile, cut the chicken meat into 1-inch strips, and divide between the serving bowls, along with the bean sprouts. Keep warm.

Add the noodles and coconut milk to the wok and simmer for 2 minutes or until the noodles are cooked. Ladle the hot noodles and broth over the shrimp, chicken, and bean sprouts. Garnish with the chopped cilantro and serve, accompanied by lime wedges.

SEARED TUNA ON JAPANESE-STYLE NOODLES

For best results and flavor, use fresh tuna rather than tuna that has been frozen. To keep the shape of the tuna while it is cooking, use it straight from the refrigerator. This dish looks most attractive when served in a bamboo steamer basket.

8 ounces thin soba noodles	Freshly ground black pepper
2 teaspoons sesame oil	2 scallions, finely chopped
1 tablespoon mirin	
12-ounce piece of tuna, about	TO SERVE
3/4 inch thick	Shredded pickled ginger
	Soy sauce

Cook the noodles in plenty of boiling water for about 4 minutes or according to the package directions. Drain and toss with half of the sesame oil. Keep warm while you cook the tuna.

Heat a skillet over high heat. The pan is hot enough if you can hold your hand over it for no more than 5 seconds. Combine the mirin and the remaining sesame oil in a small bowl, and brush over both sides of the tuna.

Place the tuna in the hot pan and press down with a spatula. Cook for 1 minute. Turn and cook on the other side for 1 minute. The tuna should be pink in the middle and well done on the edge. If you prefer, the tuna can be cooked for slightly longer. Remove from the pan, cover, and leave to rest for 1 minute.

Grind some black pepper over the tuna and put it on a carving board. Holding the fish in shape with one hand, slice it thinly with a very sharp knife.

Place the noodles on a serving platter, and arrange the tuna slices on top. Sprinkle the tuna with the scallions and serve accompanied by shredded pickled ginger and soy sauce.

SQUID WITH CHILI AND GARLIC

The texture of squid makes it very satisfying to eat. Take care not to overcook—the dish should taste zingy and fresh.

20 small squid, tentacles discarded	1 tablespoon soy sauce
4 ounces rice vermicelli noodles	1 tablespoon mirin
1 tablespoon sunflower oil	2 tablespoons bottled black bean sauce
1 teaspoon sesame oil	Pinch of sugar
2 tablespoons grated gingerroot	2 tablespoons chopped fresh cilantro
1 fresh green chili, chopped	Salt and freshly ground black pepper
2–3 garlic cloves, crushed	Lemon wedges, to serve

Cut the tapered end off each squid tube, and cut open down one side. Open out flat to form a square. Using a sharp knife, score a crisscross pattern on the inside of the squid. Set aside.

Cover the noodles with boiling water and let stand for 3 to 5 minutes or according to the package directions. Drain and keep warm.

Put the sunflower oil, sesame oil, ginger, chili, and garlic into a wok or large skillet. Cook over medium heat until the mixture is fragrant. Add the squid and stir-fry for about 5 minutes or until tender. Remove the squid and keep warm.

Add the soy sauce, mirin, black bean sauce, and sugar to the wok and boil for 2 minutes. Add the cilantro; taste and adjust the seasoning.

Spoon the squid and sauce over the noodles. Serve piping hot, garnished with lemon wedges.

Teriyaki Salmon with Noodles

MEAT NOODLES

Many of the Asian cuisines have traditional and delicious ways to make a small amount of meat go a long way,

particularly in recipes featuring noodles. With the addition of vegetables, such as bell peppers or bean sprouts, a satisfying and

nutritious meal can be prepared in next to no time. All recipes in this chapter serve 4 to 6.

MONGOLIAN HOT POT

This is a fondue-style dish, cooked at the table. The traditional cooking vessel, sometimes known as a Peking hot pot, is a round metal dish with a funnel in the middle. Hot charcoal is put into the funnel to keep the stock in the pot simmering. An electric wok or a large fondue pot are modern alternatives.

14 ounces Chinese flat wheat noodles
3 cups shredded Chinese leaves
1 pound boneless lamb, thinly sliced
10 cups beef or lamb stock

4 scallions, cut into 1-inch pieces
4 slices gingerroot
1 tablespoon soy sauce
1 bay leaf

FOR DIPPING SAUCE 1
1/2 cup soy sauce
1 scallion, finely chopped
1 garlic clove, crushed
1 tablespoon sunflower oil

FOR DIPPING SAUCE 2
6 tablespoons wine vinegar
1-inch piece gingerroot, finely chopped
1 teaspoon shredded pickled ginger

FOR DIPPING SAUCE 3
6 tablespoons peanut butter
2 tablespoons sesame oil
2 tablespoons water

1 tablespoon soy sauce
1 tablespoon bottled chili sauce

First make the dipping sauces. Mix together the ingredients for each sauce, and transfer to serving bowls.

Cook the noodles in boiling water for 2 minutes, just to blanch. Drain and arrange on a platter with the Chinese leaves. Arrange the thinly sliced lamb on another platter.

Bring most of the stock to a simmer and pour into the hot pot, wok, or fondue pot. Add the scallions, ginger, soy sauce, and bay leaf. Return to a simmer.

Each person uses chopsticks or a fondue fork to take pieces of lamb and cook them in the simmering stock for about 30 seconds. The lamb should then be dipped into one of the sauces before eating.

After the stock has been flavored by the lamb, the noodles and Chinese leaves are either dipped and cooked by each person, or added to the hot pot with any remaining stock and cooked to make a tasty soup.

RED BEEF NOODLES

For any cook new to preparing Asian food, a spice grinder is a useful piece of equipment. Freshly ground spices, as used in this recipe, have more flavor and pungency than the commercial variety.

4 red bell peppers, halved, seeded and cored
1 1/4 pounds fresh udon noodles
1 tablespoon sunflower oil
2 teaspoons yellow mustard seeds

1 pound sirloin steak, cut into strips
3/8 inch wide
Fresh red basil leaves, to garnish

FOR THE SPICE PASTE
1 tablespoon coriander seeds
2 garlic cloves, crushed
2-inch piece gingerroot, shredded
1 tablespoon sugar
1 tablespoon soy sauce

2 teaspoons sesame oil
2 tablespoons tomato paste
2 teaspoons rice vinegar
1 teaspoon cayenne pepper
2 tablespoons sesame seeds

First make the spice paste. Grind the coriander seeds, garlic, and ginger together using a mortar and pestle or in a spice grinder. Add the sugar, soy sauce, sesame oil, tomato paste, rice vinegar, cayenne, and sesame seeds. Set aside to infuse.

Preheat the oven to 350°F/180°C. Roast the peppers for 30 minutes or until the skins are blistered. (Alternatively, broil under a medium-high broiler for 15 minutes.) Put into a plastic bag, or cover with damp paper towels, and leave until cool enough to handle. Peel off and discard the skin and finely chop the flesh of the peppers.

Cook the noodles in plenty of boiling water for 2 minutes or according to the package directions. Drain.

Heat the oil in a wok or large skillet over medium heat. Add the mustard seeds and cover the pan immediately. The seeds will pop in the hot oil; when the popping has subsided, remove the lid.

Add the spice paste and stir-fry until it is fragrant. Increase the heat, add the chopped red pepper and stir-fry for 1 minute. Add the strips of beef and stir-fry over high heat for 2 minutes or until the beef is just cooked through. Spoon the mixture over the noodles, garnish with red basil leaves, and serve immediately.

Char Sui Noodles

SWEET PORK NOODLES

An unusual and filling recipe from Thailand.

1 pound boneless pork tenderloin
³/₄ cup bottled fish sauce
Generous ¹/₃ cup soft brown sugar
5 ounces rice thread noodles
1 tablespoon sunflower oil
3 scallions, sliced

2 kaffir lime leaves, shredded
1 fresh green chili, seeded and sliced
¹/₂ stalk lemongrass, finely chopped
2 tablespoons soy sauce
Fresh red basil leaves, to garnish

Remove the rind from the pork, and put both rind and meat into a saucepan with cold water to cover. Add ¹/₂ cup of the fish sauce and the brown sugar, and bring to a boil. Skim any foam from the surface. Cover and simmer over low heat for 1 hour, skimming occasionally. At the end of this time the rind should be translucent.

Drain the pork and rind and set aside to cool. About 20 minutes before serving, slice the pork and rind into thin shreds.

Pour boiling water over the noodles and let stand for 5 minutes or according to the package directions. Drain well and set aside.

Heat the oil in a wok or large skillet over medium-high heat. Add the scallions, lime leaves, chili, and lemongrass and stir-fry for 2 minutes. Add the shredded pork and rind and stir-fry over high heat for 5 minutes. Add the soy sauce, the remaining fish sauce, and the drained noodles. Use two spoons to lift and stir until the noodles are evenly coated and hot through. Serve immediately, garnished with the red basil leaves.

CHAR SUI NOODLES

A sophisticated Chinese recipe, which requires a little more attention than quick stir-frying.

2 tablespoons light soy sauce
1 tablespoon honey
1 garlic clove, crushed
1 tablespoon dry sherry
2 tablespoons bottled hoisin sauce
2 tablespoons bottled oyster sauce
1 tablespoon sugar
2 tablespoons sunflower oil

1 teaspoon star anise seeds, crushed
12 ounces pork tenderloin, in one piece
7 ounces flat rice noodles
1¹/₂ cups finely shredded spinach
or pak choi
2 scallions, cut into 1-inch pieces and
shredded lengthwise
Fresh cilantro, to garnish

Combine the soy sauce, honey, garlic, sherry, hoisin sauce, oyster sauce, sugar, oil, and star anise. Cut the pork tenderloin in half lengthwise and smear with the soy mixture, rubbing it well into the meat. Leave to marinate for up to 1 hour.

Preheat the oven to 425°F/220°C. Place the pork in a small roasting pan and roast for 4 to 8 minutes. Baste with the pan juices and return to the oven. Reduce the temperature to 350°F/180°C and roast for 4 to 8 minutes longer or until the pork is just cooked in the middle, but still moist.

Meanwhile, cook the noodles in boiling water for 3 to 5 minutes or according to the package directions. Stir the spinach and scallions into the boiling water with the noodles, then drain and keep warm.

Brush the pork with any remaining marinade, then slice neatly, using a very sharp knife.

Divide the cooked noodles and spinach between the serving plates and top with the slices of pork. Garnish with cilantro and serve.

HEARTY BEEF NOODLES

A great pick-me-up or a nourishing lunch dish. Beef marrow is available from the supermarket meat counter at little or no cost.

8 ounces medium egg noodles
2 ounces beef marrow
4 shallots, sliced

4 tablespoons dry sherry
2 tablespoons chopped fresh parsley
Salt and freshly ground black pepper

TO GARNISH
Lemon wedges
2 tablespoons snipped fresh chives

Cook the noodles in boiling water for 5 minutes or according to the package directions. Drain well and set aside.

Melt the beef marrow in a wok or large skillet over medium heat. Add the shallots and stir-fry for 1 minute or until the shallots soften. Add the sherry and bring to a boil. Immediately add the noodles and parsley. Use two spoons to lift and stir until the noodles are evenly coated and hot through. Season generously and serve immediately, garnished with lemon wedges and snipped chives.

SPICED PORK

Pork is widely used in Oriental cookery. In this recipe, it takes on a rich, smoky taste from the spice mix.

1 pound boneless pork tenderloin
1 tablespoon cloves
5 tablespoons rice wine
3 tablespoons tomato paste
1 teaspoon black peppercorns, crushed
Salt
1 cinnamon stick, crushed
1 teaspoon star anise seeds, ground
2 tablespoons sunflower oil
1 leek, cut into small strips
2 carrots, cut into matchsticks
7 ounces flat rice noodles
4 tablespoons chopped fresh cilantro

Make nicks all over the pork and insert the cloves. Put the pork into a bowl just large enough to accommodate it.

Combine the rice wine, tomato paste, peppercorns, a little salt, the cinnamon, and star anise in a saucepan. Heat through without boiling. Spoon the mixture over the pork, rubbing it well into the flesh. Let cool completely, then refrigerate for 4 hours, basting often.

Preheat the oven to 350°F/180°C. Heat the oil in a wok or heavy skillet over medium-high heat. Add the pork (reserve the marinade) and seal on all sides. Transfer to a small roasting pan and roast for 25 minutes or until tender.

Meanwhile, make the sauce. Pour the reserved marinade into a saucepan and stir in the leek and carrots. Bring to a boil and simmer for 5 minutes, adding a little water if needed.

Pour boiling water over the noodles and let stand for 10 minutes or according to the package directions. Drain and keep warm.

Slice the pork. Stir the cilantro into the sauce and add any juices from the roasting pan. Taste and adjust the seasoning. Divide the noodles between serving plates, top with the pork and sauce. and serve.

CANTONESE BEEF NOODLES

The Cantonese are known for their love of food, such as this stir-fried beef with a rich oyster sauce.

12 ounces top round beef
1 tablespoon freshly grated gingerroot
4 garlic cloves, finely sliced
3 tablespoons bottled oyster sauce
2 tablespoons soy sauce
1 teaspoon chili oil
Salt and freshly ground black pepper
12 ounces Chinese flat wheat noodles or flat rice noodles
2 teaspoons sesame oil
2 scallions, chopped
1 large green bell pepper, chopped

Slice the beef across the grain into 1¹/₄ x ³/₈-inch strips. Put into a bowl with the ginger, garlic, oyster sauce, soy sauce, and chili oil. Season with salt and pepper and leave to marinate for 30 minutes.

Cook the noodles in plenty of boiling water for 5 minutes or according to the package directions. Drain well and keep warm.

Heat the sesame oil in a wok or large skillet. Add the scallions and green pepper and stir-fry for 30 seconds. Add the beef and its marinade and stir-fry over high heat for 4 minutes. Taste and adjust the seasoning. Serve hot, spooned over the noodles.

HOT–AND–SOUR PORK NOODLES

Hot–and–sour sauces are perennial favorites. Here, cubes of pork are added, and served over fine beancurd noodles.

6 ounces beancurd noodles
2 tablespoons sunflower oil
1 pound boneless pork, cut into
1-inch cubes
2 garlic cloves, crushed
1-inch piece gingerroot, shredded
2 fresh red chilies, seeded and sliced
¹/₂ cup finely chopped pineapple, fresh or packed in natural juice
3 tablespoons rice vinegar
3 tablespoons bottled yellow bean sauce
1 tablespoon soy sauce
Pinch of sugar
1 tablespoon lemon juice
2 scallions, sliced, to garnish

Pour boiling water over the noodles and let stand for 5 minutes or according to the package directions. Drain and keep warm.

Heat the oil in a wok or large skillet. Add the pork, garlic, ginger, and red chilies and stir-fry for 2 minutes. Add the pineapple, rice vinegar, and yellow bean sauce and stir-fry over high heat until the sauce dries out slightly, about 1 minute. Add the soy sauce and sugar to taste, then remove from the heat and sprinkle with the lemon juice.

Arrange the noodles on serving plates and top with the pork mixture. Serve immediately, garnished with the sliced scallions.

Hot–and–Sour Pork Noodles

47

PORK BALLS

An Oriental version of spaghetti and meatballs, in a sweet-sour sauce.

1 pound ground pork	4 tablespoons sugar
1 tablespoon dry sherry	6 tablespoons garlic-flavored vinegar
1 teaspoon salt	6 tablespoons tomato paste
1 egg, lightly beaten	6 tablespoons orange juice
3 scallions, finely chopped	1 1/2 cups finely chopped pineapple, fresh or
1 teaspoon ground coriander	packed in natural juice
1 teaspoon ground star anise	1 1/4 cups chicken stock
1 teaspoon grated gingerroot	8 ounces egg thread noodles
3 tablespoons soy sauce	Lemon wedges, to garnish

In a large bowl, combine the pork, sherry, salt, egg, scallions, coriander, star anise, and ginger. Shape the mixture into at least 12 balls and place on a tray. Cover and chill for at least 20 minutes.

In a pan large enough to hold all of the pork balls, mix together the soy sauce, sugar, vinegar, tomato paste, orange juice, pineapple, and stock. Bring to a gentle boil. Add the pork balls and simmer for 15 minutes or until the balls are cooked through.

Meanwhile, pour boiling water over the noodles and let stand for 3 minutes or according to the package directions. Drain and keep warm.

Divide the noodles between the serving plates and spoon the pork balls and sauce over them. Serve hot, garnished with lemon wedges.

MISO RAMEN

In this healthy Japanese dish, a small quantity of beef is made to go a long way by being sliced very thinly.

1 piece of konbu, about 3 inches square	Salt and freshly ground black pepper
1/3 cup halved green beans	1 tablespoon sunflower oil
10 ounces ramen noodles	7 ounces top round of beef, thinly sliced
4 1/2 cups strong beef stock	across the grain
3 tablespoons miso paste	1/2 bunch (1 1/2 oz) watercress
2 teaspoons sesame oil	2 scallions, finely sliced
1 tablespoon mirin	1 tablespoon shredded pickled ginger
Red-pepper flakes, to taste	Wasabi paste, to serve

Soak the konbu for 15 minutes in warm water to cover. Drain and shred finely. Blanch the beans in boiling water for 1 minute. Refresh and drain. Set aside.

Pour boiling water over the noodles and let stand for 2 minutes or according to the package directions. Drain.

Heat the stock without boiling and stir in the miso, sesame oil, mirin, konbu, and pepper flakes to taste. Season well. Bring to a slow simmer.

Heat the sunflower oil in a wok or large skillet over high heat. Stir-fry the beef and beans for 1 minute or until the beef is sealed.

Divide the noodles between the serving bowls and ladle the miso stock over them. Top with the stir-fried beef and beans, followed by the watercress, scallions, and shredded pickled ginger. Serve immediately, accompanied by wasabi paste to be added to taste.

CHAR KWEE TAN

The Chinese answer to Singapore noodles, although this is a richer dish.

8 ounces flat rice noodles	1 garlic clove, crushed
1 egg	1-inch piece gingerroot, grated
1 tablespoon water	1 green bell pepper, chopped
3 tablespoons sunflower oil	6 ounces shelled raw jumbo shrimp
1 tablespoon bottled yellow bean sauce	1 can (7 oz) straw mushrooms, sliced
Pinch of salt	3/4 cup bean sprouts
8 ounces lean boneless pork, cut into	1 tablespoon dry sherry
2 x 1-inch strips	1 tablespoon light soy sauce
2 scallions, cut into 2-inch pieces	1 tablespoon dark soy sauce

Pour boiling water over the noodles and let stand for 5 minutes or according to the package directions. Drain and cut into 2-inch pieces.

Lightly beat the egg with the water. Heat 1 teaspoon of the oil in a wok or large skillet. Add the egg and swirl it around to make a very thin omelet. Remove, roll up, and let cool. When cool, slice thinly.

Heat 1 tablespoon of the oil in the wok over high heat. Add the yellow bean sauce, salt, pork, and scallions and stir-fry until the pork is just cooked, about 3 minutes. Add the noodles and stir-fry for 1 minute longer. Transfer to a baking dish, cover, and keep warm in a low oven.

Add the remaining oil, garlic, ginger, and green pepper to the wok. Stir-fry for 1 minute, then add the shrimp and stir-fry for another minute or until the shrimp turn pink. Add the mushrooms and bean sprouts and stir-fry for 3 minutes longer.

Divide the pork noodles between warmed serving plates. Top the noodles with the shrimp and vegetables, using a slotted spoon to remove them from the wok. Add the sherry and both soy sauces to the juices in the wok and stir over high heat until bubbling. Spoon onto the noodles and shrimp, garnish with strips of omelet, and serve.

BEEF TAO MEIN

A Chinese dish of noodles in a highly flavored souplike sauce.

1 tablespoon sunflower oil	5 cups beef stock
4 scallions, sliced	1 tablespoon soy sauce
1 garlic clove, crushed	2 tablespoons dry sherry
1-inch piece gingerroot, shredded	1 1/2 cups shredded pak choi
1 star anise	7 ounces Chinese flat wheat noodles or
10 ounces sirloin steak, cut into strips	flat rice noodles
1 cup halved green beans	Chili oil, to serve

Heat the oil in a wok or large skillet. Stir-fry the scallions, garlic, ginger, and star anise over medium heat for 1 minute. Add the steak, beans, stock, soy sauce, and sherry and bring to a slow boil. Add the pak choi and simmer for 4 minutes.

Meanwhile, cook the noodles in plenty of boiling water for 4 minutes or according to the package directions. Drain.

Divide the noodles between the serving bowls and ladle in the beef stew. Serve immediately, accompanied by chili oil to be added to taste.

Char Kwee Tan

CHILI BEEF RAMEN

When making this strongly flavored ramen stew, you can adjust the chili heat either by altering the quantity or by using milder chilies.

2 fresh green chilies, seeded and chopped	2 shallots, finely sliced
1 tablespoon bottled sweet chili sauce	18 ounces ramen noodles
1 tablespoon coriander seeds, crushed	5 cups strong beef stock, hot
2 garlic cloves, crushed	2 teaspoons red-pepper flakes
1/2 cup sunflower oil	3/4 cup bean sprouts
14 ounces sirloin steak, 1 inch thick and	4 tablespoons fresh cilantro leaves
in one piece	1 lime, cut into wedges

Using a mortar and pestle or a spice grinder, grind together the chilies, chili sauce, coriander seeds, garlic, and 2 tablespoon of the oil. Rub this paste all over the beef, pressing well into the flesh. Leave to marinate for up to 1 hour.

Heat the remaining oil in a wok or skillet and fry the shallots until golden and crisp. Drain on paper towels.

Pour boiling water over the noodles and let stand for 3 minutes or according to the package directions. Drain and keep warm.

Heat a wok or large skillet to searing temperature. Put the beef into the wok and press down with a spatula. Cook for 2 to 5 minutes, then turn and cook the other side for 2 to 5 minutes, pressing down firmly, until done to your liking. Remove from the wok and slice thinly.

Divide the noodles between the serving bowls, ladle in the stock, and top with the beef. Sprinkle with the fried shallots and the red-pepper flakes. Serve immediately, accompanied by the bean sprouts, cilantro leaves, and lime wedges, which can be added to taste.

BEEF CHOW MEIN

Chow mein is many people's first experience of Oriental noodles, and it is so delicious it usually makes them want more.

2 tablespoons soy sauce	1 teaspoon sesame oil
5 tablespoons bottled hoisin sauce	3 scallions, sliced diagonally
Freshly ground black pepper	1-inch piece gingerroot, shredded
1 pound top round beef, thinly sliced	1 red bell pepper, diced
across the grain	2 tablespoons rice wine or dry sherry
8 ounces chow mein noodles	1/2 cup strong beef stock
2 tablespoons vegetable oil	

Combine the soy sauce and hoisin sauce in a bowl. Season generously with freshly ground pepper. Add the meat strips and leave to marinate for up to 1 hour, but no longer, or the soy sauce will toughen the meat.

Cook the noodles in plenty of boiling water according to the package directions. Drain and set aside.

Heat both oils in a wok or large skillet over high heat. Stir-fry the scallions, ginger, and red pepper for 1 minute. Add the meat and the marinade and stir-fry for 2 minutes. Add the noodles, and stir in the rice wine and stock. Use two spoons to lift and stir the noodles until they are evenly coated and hot through. Serve immediately.

PORK SOBA

You don't need much pork for this dish, which includes flavorsome soba noodles and crunchy .

1 teaspoon freshly ground black pepper	1 1/2 cups bean sprouts
1 tablespoon light soy sauce	2 scallions, finely sliced
1 tablespoon lemon juice	
12 ounces pork tenderloin, in one piece	TO GARNISH
10 ounces soba noodles	1-inch piece gingerroot, shredded
5 cups strong chicken stock, hot	1 fresh red chili, sliced

Combine the pepper, soy sauce, and lemon juice, and spoon over the pork, rubbing well into the flesh. Leave to marinate for 1 hour.

Cook the noodles in plenty of boiling water for 3 minutes or according to the package directions. Drain and keep warm.

Heat a heavy-bottomed skillet. When it is quite hot, put in the pork and press down with a spatula. Cover the pan and cook for 4 to 8 minutes. Turn the pork over and cook for 4 to 8 minutes on the other side or until cooked to your liking. Remove the pork and let rest for 1 minute, then slice thinly.

Ladle the noodles and hot stock into bowls, and add the bean sprouts, scallions, and pork. Garnish with ginger and red chili, and serve.

FILIPINO PORK

The ingredients here may seem unusual, but they work very well. Tomato ketchup is widely used as a flavoring in Asia.

1 can fizzy lemon-lime soda, or	4 boneless pork loin chops
carbonated lemonade	7 ounces rice thread noodles
2 tablespoons gin	1 tablespoon sunflower oil
5 tablespoons tomato ketchup	1 fresh green chili, seeded and finely
2 teaspoons garlic salt	chopped
1 tablespoon Worcestershire sauce	2 scallions, sliced
Salt and freshly ground black pepper	

Combine the lemon-lime drink, gin, tomato ketchup, garlic salt, Worcestershire sauce, and seasoning in a large, nonporous dish. Add the pork chops and turn them in the marinade. Refrigerate for about 2 hours. Remove from the refrigerator 30 minutes before cooking.

Preheat the oven to 350°F/180°C. Transfer the pork chops to a roasting pan and roast for 4 minutes. Baste with the pan juices, cover, and cook for 15 minutes longer.

Meanwhile, cook the noodles in plenty of boiling water according to the package directions. Drain and toss with the oil. Stir the green chili and scallions through the noodles.

To serve, divide the noodles between the serving plates. Slice the pork chops into 6 pieces each and arrange on top of the noodles.

Chili Beef Ramen

VEGETABLES

From a classic Japanese dish of crisp tempura vegetables and noodles in broth, to Chinese chow mein, to a meat-free version of Thai green curry, this chapter contains many ideas to stimulate the palates of vegetarians and meat-eaters alike. Some are substantial vegetarian main meals, while others are imaginative side dishes. All recipes in this chapter serve 4 to 6.

CHILI NOODLES

These noodles are just spicy enough for most tastes, and are delicious with a mild curry or any sweet hot dish.

2 shallots	1/2 teaspoon salt
2 garlic cloves	8 ounces egg thread noodles
2 small fresh red chilies	2 tablespoons sunflower oil
2-inch piece gingerroot, roughly chopped	1 tablespoon water

Put the shallots, garlic, chilies, ginger, and salt into a food processor, and blend to a smooth paste.

Pour boiling water over the noodles and let stand for 4 minutes or according to the package directions. Drain.

Heat the oil in a wok and stir in the paste. Stir-fry for 1 to 2 minutes, until fragrant. Add the water and the noodles, mix with the paste until they are well coated, and stir-fry for 3 minutes. Serve immediately.

STIR-FRIED UDON NOODLES

Udon noodles are fantastic stir-fried, making a really satisfying dish that is a meal in itself. If you cannot find fresh noodles, use dried; cook them first in boiling water according to the package directions.

1 1/4 pounds fresh udon noodles	1 tablespoon light soy sauce
3 scallions, roughly chopped	Pinch of sugar
1 1/2 cups bean sprouts	4 teaspoons sunflower oil
2 cups sliced shiitake mushrooms	
1 red bell pepper, chopped	TO GARNISH
1 garlic clove, crushed	Scallion, finely sliced
1-inch piece gingerroot, grated	Japanese seven-pepper spice or
1 tablespoon mirin	lemon pepper
1 teaspoon chili oil	Pickled ginger or radish

In a large bowl, combine the udon noodles, scallions, bean sprouts, shiitake mushrooms, and red pepper.

In a small bowl, combine the garlic, ginger, mirin, chili oil, soy sauce, sugar, and 1 teaspoon of the sunflower oil.

Heat the remaining oil in a wok or large skillet. When it is very hot, add the noodle mixture and stir-fry over high heat for 3 minutes. Add the soy mixture and use two spoons to lift and stir so the noodles and vegetables are coated with the sauce.

Transfer to a heated serving dish, garnish with the scallion, pepper, and pickle, and serve immediately.

INDONESIAN SPICED NOODLES

These highly aromatic noodles are known as *bami goreng* in their native Indonesia.

2 kaffir lime leaves, finely shredded	8 ounces egg thread noodles
1/2 stalk lemongrass, finely chopped	3 tablespoons sunflower oil
3 fresh red chilies, chopped	3 shallots, sliced
2 garlic cloves, roughly chopped	1-inch piece gingerroot, grated
2 cloves	2-inch piece galangal, grated
2 teaspoons coriander seeds	Juice of 1 lime
1/2 teaspoon tamarind pulp, or	2 tablespoons roughly chopped natural
2 teaspoons tamarind juice (page 5)	peanuts, roasted
2 teaspoons soft brown sugar	Indonesian soy sauce (kecap manis),
2 teaspoons turmeric	to serve
1 teaspoon ground cinnamon	

Grind together the lime leaves, lemongrass, red chilies, garlic, cloves, and coriander seeds using a mortar and pestle or in a spice grinder to make a paste. Transfer to a small bowl and stir in the tamarind, brown sugar, turmeric, and ground cinnamon.

Put the noodles in a large bowl and cover with boiling water. Let stand for 3 minutes or according to the package directions. Drain well.

Heat the oil in a wok or large skillet. Add the shallots and cook over low heat for 10 minutes or until they are soft. Increase the heat, add the ginger and galangal, and stir-fry for 1 minute. Add the spice paste and stir-fry until fragrant.

Add the lime juice and noodles and cook for 4 to 5 minutes, using two spoons to lift and stir so the noodles are evenly coated.

Transfer to a serving dish and sprinkle with the peanuts. Serve immediately, accompanied by *kecap manis*.

THAI STIR-FRY NOODLES

A wonderful combination of flavors and textures makes this a very special dish. It looks good, too, with spicy noodles and beansprouts rolled up inside a thin omelet and garnished with deep-fried peanuts, tofu, and shrimp.

2/3 cup sunflower oil
2 heaped tablespoons natural peanuts, sliced
2 heaped tablespoons diced firm tofu
2 tablespoons dried shrimp
8 ounces rice thread noodles
2 dried red chilies, seeded and finely ground
1 shallot, finely chopped
1 garlic clove, crushed

4 tablespoons fish sauce
1 tablespoon soft brown sugar
2 teaspoons tamarind juice (page 5)
Juice of 1 lime
1 1/2 cups bean sprouts
2 eggs
2 tablespoons water
3 tablespoons chopped fresh cilantro

Heat the oil in a wok or large skillet and deep-fry the peanuts until golden brown. Drain on paper towels. Deep-fry the tofu and then the dried shrimp. Drain and set aside. Keep the oil in the wok.

Put the noodles in a large bowl and cover with boiling water. Let stand for 3 minutes or according to the package directions. Drain well.

Pour off all but 2 tablespoons of oil from the wok. Add the red chilies, shallot, garlic, fish sauce, brown sugar, tamarind, and lime juice. Stir-fry this spice paste until it is fragrant. Add the bean sprouts and noodles, and use two spoons to lift and stir the noodles until evenly coated. Transfer to a baking dish, cover, and keep warm in a low oven.

Lightly beat the eggs with the water. Pour into the hot wok and swirl around the pan to make a large, thin omelet. Turn out onto a plate.

Spread the noodles over the omelet, sprinkle with the cilantro, and roll it up. Set on a warmed serving plate and garnish with the fried peanuts, tofu, and dried shrimp.

CHOW MEIN

In China, this popular dish will vary according to who makes it and which vegetables are in season. Very few Chinese recipes are written down, and versions of the same dish vary widely.

4 dried Chinese mushrooms, or fresh shiitake mushrooms
14 ounces chow mein noodles
5 tablespoons vegetable stock
1 tablespoon soy sauce
1 tablespoon bottled oyster sauce
1 tablespoon bottled hoisin sauce

2 tablespoons dry sherry
1 tablespoon sunflower oil
2 scallions, sliced
1 garlic clove, crushed
2 ounces canned bamboo shoots, drained
8 canned water chestnuts, sliced
2 cups bean sprouts

If using dried Chinese mushrooms, soak them in warm water for 15 minutes. Drain, and remove and discard the stems and slice the caps. If using fresh shiitake mushrooms, slice them. Set aside.

Cook the noodles in plenty of boiling water according to the package directions. Drain well and set aside.

Combine the vegetable stock, soy sauce, oyster sauce, hoisin sauce, and sherry in a bowl and set aside.

Heat the oil in a large wok over medium-high heat. Add the scallions and garlic and stir-fry for 1 minute. Add the mushrooms, bamboo shoots, and water chestnuts and stir-fry over high heat for 1 minute longer. Add the bean sprouts and sauce mixture and stir until well combined. Simmer for 2 minutes or until the sauce thickens slightly.

Add the noodles to the wok and heat through, using two spoons to lift and stir until the noodles are evenly coated. Serve piping hot.

SPINACH NOODLES

An attractive and appealing combination of broccoli, spinach, and egg noodles, with sliced water chestnuts adding an unexpected crunch.

1 chicken stock cube
8 ounces medium egg noodles
1 1/2 cups broccoli florets
1 tablespoon sunflower oil

18 ounces fresh spinach
1 can (7 oz) water chestnuts, drained and sliced
Salt and freshly ground black pepper

Bring a large pan of water to a boil and crumble in the stock cube. Add the noodles and cook for 4 to 5 minutes or according to the package directions. Drain well and set aside.

Blanch the broccoli florets in boiling water; drain well and keep warm.

Heat the oil in a wok or large skillet. Add the spinach and stir-fry until wilted, about 5 minutes. Stir in the broccoli florets. Add the water chestnuts and stir-fry for 1 minute. Stir in the noodles and cook, using two spoons to lift and mix until heated through. Season to taste and serve immediately.

YELLOW PEPPER NOODLES

These look stunning! The sweet yellow bell pepper sauce is the perfect foil for robust soba noodles.

6 yellow bell peppers	*Salt and freshly ground black pepper*
1 whole head of garlic	*10 ounces soba noodles*
2 tablespoons olive oil	*Fresh red basil, to garnish*

Preheat the oven to 400°F/200°C. Cut the yellow peppers in half lengthwise and remove the seeds and white ribs. Put the pepper halves on a baking tray with the garlic head and bake for 30 minutes. Squeeze the garlic; if it does not yield easily to pressure, return to the oven for 20 minutes longer or so. Put the peppers and garlic into a plastic bag, or cover with damp paper towels, and set aside to cool.

When cool enough to handle, peel the peppers and set aside. Cut the top off the garlic to expose the soft cloves. Squeeze the cloves into a food processor or bowl, and blend or mash together with the yellow peppers. Stir in the olive oil and season generously.

Heat the yellow pepper sauce through gently in a small saucepan or in the microwave.

Meanwhile, cook the noodles in plenty of boiling water according to the package directions. Drain. To serve, toss the noodles with the sauce and garnish with red basil.

KITSUNE UDON

Tofu, or soybean curd, has been eaten in Japan, China, and Thailand for centuries. It is an excellent source of protein, and readily absorbs the flavors of other ingredients.

3¹/2 ounces firm tofu	*2 tablespoons light soy sauce*
8¹/2 cups dashi broth	*1 teaspoon soft brown sugar*
4 tablespoons dark soy sauce	*1 tablespoon sake or dry sherry*
1 tablespoon sugar	*Salt*
7 ounces udon noodles	*1 tablespoon hijiki, soaked in warm water*
4 scallions, thinly sliced diagonally	*for 10 minutes*

Bring a pan of water to a boil. Add the tofu, bring back to a boil, and drain immediately and cut into small cubes.

Combine 1³/4 cups of the dashi broth, 2 tablespoons of the dark soy sauce, and the sugar in a small saucepan. Bring to a boil. Add the tofu cubes and simmer for 5 minutes. Drain and discard the cooking liquid.

Cook the noodles in plenty of boiling water for 5 minutes or according to the package directions. Put the scallions in a small wire strainer and dip briefly into the boiling water; refresh under cold running water, and set aside. Drain the noodles, rinse, and drain again.

Put the remaining dashi broth and dark soy sauce in a saucepan with the light soy sauce, brown sugar, and sake or sherry. Bring to a boil and season to taste with salt.

Arrange the noodles in the serving bowls and top with the tofu, scallions, and drained hijiki. Ladle in the hot broth and serve immediately.

MUSHROOM NOODLES

You can use any mixture of fresh or dried mushrooms, according to what is available.

2 scallions	*1 cup sliced or halved oyster mushrooms*
2 tablespoons sunflower oil	*¹/2 ounce dried porcini mushrooms, soaked*
1 garlic clove, unpeeled and lightly crushed	*in warm water for 15 minutes and drained*
1¹/2 cups quartered field or button	*Light soy sauce, to taste*
mushrooms	*8 ounces egg thread noodles*
1 cup sliced shiitake mushrooms	

Cut the scallions into 2-inch pieces and slice each piece lengthwise very finely.

Heat the oil with the garlic in a wok or large skillet. Add the scallions and field mushrooms and stir. Add the shiitake mushrooms, followed by the oyster mushrooms. Stir again, then add the porcini. Stir-fry the mushrooms until fragrant. Season with soy sauce.

Put the noodles in a large bowl and cover with boiling water. Let stand for 3 minutes or according to the package directions, then drain.

Pile the noodles on a serving plate. Discard the garlic clove, and spoon the mushrooms and all the pan juices over the noodles. Serve hot.

Yellow Pepper Noodles

55

GREEN NOODLES

The fresh taste of cilantro really comes to the fore in this recipe. You can make the sauce in advance—it will keep for 3 to 5 days in the refrigerator—and reheat it while you cook the noodles.

1 garlic clove	2 scallions, roughly chopped
1 teaspoon salt	1 fresh red chili, seeded and sliced
1 tablespoon black peppercorns	3 tablespoons lemon juice
2 ounces fresh cilantro, including stems and any root	2/3 cup coconut milk
2 tablespoons chopped fresh parsley, preferably flat-leaf	2 tablespoons peanut butter
	8 ounces flat rice noodles
	Lemon quarters, to serve

To make the sauce, grind the garlic, salt, peppercorns, and cilantro together using a mortar and pestle, or in a blender, or spice grinder. Add the parsley, scallions, and chili, and grind to a rough paste.

Transfer the paste to a saucepan and stir in the lemon juice, coconut milk, and peanut butter. Bring to a slow boil, stirring occasionally.

Meanwhile, put the noodles in a large bowl and cover with boiling water. Let stand for 5 minutes or according to the package directions. Drain well.

Toss the noodles with the sauce until they are evenly coated. Serve immediately, with lemon quarters.

DANDAN NOODLES

Also known as "beggars' noodles," these make a great meat-free meal. The nuts add heaps of flavor.

1 teaspoon chili oil	1/2 cup natural peanuts
1 garlic clove, crushed	6 cups strong chicken stock
4 tablespoons smooth peanut butter	2 cups roughly chopped pickled Chinese cabbage
4 tablespoons light soy sauce	
2 tablespoons soft brown sugar	8 ounces medium egg noodles
1 tablespoon balsamic or Chinese vinegar	2 teaspoons sesame oil
2 tablespoons sunflower oil	4 scallions, finely sliced
5 dried red chilies	

Combine the chili oil, garlic, peanut butter, soy sauce, brown sugar, and vinegar in a bowl. Whisk well and set aside.

Heat the sunflower oil in a wok or large skillet. Add the chilies and stir-fry until crisp. Drain on paper towels. Fry the peanuts in the same oil until golden, and drain on paper towels.

Bring the chicken stock to a slow boil in a saucepan. Add half the pickled cabbage, cover, and simmer for 2 minutes only. Keep hot.

Put the noodles in a large bowl and cover with boiling water. Let stand for 2 minutes only. Drain well and toss with the sesame oil.

Arrange the noodles in warmed serving bowls. Whisk the sauce again and spoon it over the noodles. Ladle in the hot stock. Serve immediately, accompanied by the scallions, fried chilies, and peanuts, and the remaining pickled cabbage, to be added to taste.

THAI SPICED NOODLES

All the traditional flavors of Thai food are highlighted in this dish, each complementing the light texture of the noodles.

8 ounces flat rice noodles	1/4 cup roughly chopped natural peanuts
3 tablespoons sunflower oil	1 teaspoon soft brown sugar
1 teaspoon sesame oil	1 cup fresh chives cut into short pieces
1/2 stalk lemongrass, finely chopped	5 tablespoons lime juice
2 garlic cloves, sliced	
1 teaspoon shredded pickled radish	TO SERVE
4 cups bean sprouts	Chopped fresh cilantro
2 tablespoons Indonesian soy sauce	Lime wedges
2 tablespoons fish sauce	Red-pepper flakes

Put the noodles in a large bowl and cover with boiling water. Let stand for 5 minutes or according to the package directions. Drain well.

Heat the sunflower oil and sesame oil in a wok. Add the chopped lemongrass and stir-fry over medium heat for 2 minutes or until the lemongrass is tender. Add the garlic and pickled radish and stir-fry over high heat until brown.

Add the noodles and half the bean sprouts and mix well. Stir in the soy sauce, fish sauce, peanuts, and sugar. Stir-fry over medium-high heat for 2 minutes, using two spoons to lift and stir until the noodles are evenly coated and heated through. Add the chives, and transfer to a serving plate.

Top with the remaining bean sprouts and sprinkle with the lime juice. Serve accompanied by the cilantro, lime wedges, and red-pepper flakes, to be added to taste.

Green Noodles

Sesame Noodles with Cabbage

This noodle dish is an excellent accompaniment to simply cooked pork or chicken dishes.

7 ounces egg thread noodles	7 cups finely shredded Savoy cabbage
2 teaspoons sesame oil	1 tablespoon soy sauce
2 tablespoons sunflower oil	3 tablespoons sesame seeds, toasted

Cook the noodles in plenty of boiling water for 4 minutes or according to the package directions. Drain well and set aside.

Heat the sesame oil and sunflower oil in a wok or large skillet. Add the cabbage and stir-fry for 6 to 7 minutes or until the cabbage is tender to the bite. Stir in the soy sauce.

Add the noodles to the wok and stir-fry with the cabbage for about 2 minutes, lifting and mixing with two spoons. Add the sesame seeds, stir, and serve immediately.

Sichuan Spiced Noodles

The Sichuan province of western China has a very mild climate, and vegetables grow in abundance. Spicy hot and salty flavorings are used a great deal there, and although noodles are not widely eaten in western China, the Sichuan flavorings suit noodles very well.

1 tablespoon Sichuan peppercorns	1 tablespoon sesame oil
3 tablespoons roughly chopped gingerroot	1 tablespoon sunflower oil
3 star anise seeds	Juice of 1 lime
1/2 teaspoon ground cinnamon	1 tablespoon rice vinegar or cider vinegar
3 cloves	Pinch of sugar
2 scallions, finely chopped	3/4 cup chopped fresh cilantro
1 1/2 tablespoons honey	8 ounces medium egg noodles
3 tablespoons light soy sauce	7 ounces mustard greens or other
1 tablespoon dry sherry	Chinese greens

Place the Sichuan peppercorns, ginger, star anise, cinnamon, cloves, and scallions in a blender, mortar and pestle, or spice grinder and grind to a rough paste. Transfer to a bowl and add the honey, soy sauce, sherry, sesame oil, sunflower oil, lime juice, vinegar, and sugar. Stir in the chopped cilantro.

Put the noodles in a large bowl and cover with boiling water. Let stand for 5 minutes or according to the package directions. Drain well.

Heat a wok or large skillet. Add the spice paste and stir-fry until fragrant. Add the noodles and use two spoons to lift and stir the noodles until they are evenly coated in sauce and hot through. Remove to a warmed serving platter.

Stir-fry the greens in the pan juices, and spoon over the noodles. Serve immediately.

Stuffed Peppers

Rice vermicelli noodles are great for stuffing vegetables. Here they are combined with cucumber, coriander seeds, and garlic, and spooned into baked red bell pepper halves.

4 red bell peppers	1 teaspoon sesame oil
3 1/2 ounces rice vermicelli noodles	2 garlic cloves, crushed
1/2 cucumber, peeled and chopped	About 1 tablespoon soy sauce
1 tablespoon coriander seeds, crushed	2 tablespoons sesame seeds, toasted
1 tablespoon sunflower oil	

Preheat the oven to 350°F/180°C. Leaving the stems on the peppers, cut them in half lengthwise and remove the seeds and white ribs. Arrange the pepper halves on a baking tray and cover with foil. Bake for 15 minutes.

While the noodles are still in the package, break them up into small pieces. Put the noodles in a large bowl and cover with boiling water. Let stand for 3 minutes or according to the package directions. Drain well and set aside.

Mix together the cucumber and coriander seeds.

Heat the sunflower oil and sesame oil in a wok or large skillet. Add the garlic and stir-fry for 1 minute over medium-high heat. Add the cucumber and coriander mixture and stir-fry for about 2 minutes. Add the noodles and use two spoons to lift and toss the noodles until they are coated with the mixture and hot through. Season to taste with the soy sauce.

Put two pepper halves on each serving plate, fill with the noodle mixture, and serve hot, garnished with the sesame seeds.

Noodles on the Side

A versatile side dish, this is excellent with a curry or any fried dish.

14 ounces rice noodles, flat or vermicelli
3 1/2 tablespoons lime juice
2 fresh red chilies, seeded and chopped

Cook the noodles in plenty of boiling water, either in a pan or by soaking, according to the package directions. Drain.

Toss the hot noodles with the lime juice and chopped chili; serve hot.

LAYERED CRISPY NOODLES

Baked winter vegetables are given an Oriental touch with yellow bean sauce, then sandwiched between deep-fried noodle pancakes.

²/₃ cup peeled and cubed pumpkin	*2 tablespoons butter*
1 carrot, cubed	*3¹/₂ ounces egg thread noodles*
1 turnip, cubed	*3 tablespoons bottled yellow bean sauce*
1 leek, diced	*2 scallions, finely sliced*
1 tablespoon sunflower oil	*Vegetable oil for deep-frying*
1 garlic clove, crushed	*Chopped fresh cilantro, to garnish*
Salt and freshly ground black pepper	

Preheat the oven to 350°F/180°C. Mix together the pumpkin, carrot, turnip, and leek in a baking dish, and stir in the oil and garlic. Season well and dot with the butter. Cover and bake for 1 hour or until the vegetables are tender.

Meanwhile, put the noodles in a large bowl and cover with boiling water. Let stand for 3 minutes or according to the package directions, then drain well. Divide the noodles into 12 portions and spread each into a flat pancake shape, about 4 inches across, on a tray or the countertop. Leave to dry completely.

When the vegetables are perfectly tender, reduce the oven heat to very low. Coat the vegetables with the yellow bean sauce and stir in the scallions. Keep warm in the low oven while you fry the noodles.

Heat 2 inches of oil in a wok or large skillet to about 350°F/180°C. Place a noodle pancake on a wire draining spoon and slip it into the oil, being careful to keep its shape. Fry, turning once, until golden brown all over. Drain on paper towels and season generously with salt. Fry the remaining noodle pancakes in the same way.

To serve, sandwich the vegetable mixture between pairs of fried noodle pancakes and sprinkle liberally with cilantro.

LEMON AND PARSLEY NOODLES

This flavoring is based on the Mediterranean gremolata mixture.

2 tablespoons grated lemon zest	*Salt*
2 tablespoons finely chopped fresh parsley	*Noodles of your choice*
1 teaspoon freshly ground black pepper	*1 tablespoon lemon juice*

Combine the lemon zest, parsley, black pepper, and salt to taste.

Cook the noodles according to the package directions. Drain and immediately toss with the lemon juice, followed by the lemon zest mixture. Serve hot.

GREEN CURRIED NOODLES

This is a version of the classic Thai green curry. It can be served without the vegetables if you prefer just a flavored noodle dish.

8 ounces flat rice noodles	*FOR THE SPICE PASTE*
1 tablespoon sunflower oil	*1-inch piece galangal, chopped*
2 ounces green beans, blanched	*1 teaspoon coriander seeds*
2 zucchini, diced	*¹/₂ teaspoon black peppercorns*
1 cup coconut milk	*3 cloves*
4 ounces fresh Thai spinach, or	*1 stalk lemongrass, roughly chopped*
ordinary spinach	*4 tablespoons chopped fresh cilantro*
Juice of 1 lime	*3 garlic cloves*
2 tablespoons shredded fresh basil	*2 shallots, chopped*
1 tablespoon chopped fresh cilantro	*6 fresh green chilies, seeded*
1 tablespoon chopped fresh mint	*1 teaspoon shrimp paste*
	2 kaffir lime leaves

To make the spice paste, grind all the ingredients together using a large mortar and pestle or in a spice grinder. Set aside.

Put the noodles in a large bowl, cover with boiling water, and let stand for 3 minutes or according to the package directions. Drain well.

Heat the oil in a wok and add the spice paste. Stir-fry until fragrant. Add the beans and zucchini and stir-fry over medium heat for 1 minute. Add the coconut milk and bring to a slow boil. Stir in the noodles and spinach. Sprinkle in the lime juice, basil, cilantro, and mint. Serve immediately.

Green Curried Noodles

MOYASHI SOBA

Although this vegetarian dish is historically misnamed "soba" by the Japanese, it uses ramen noodles.

2-inch piece daikon, finely shredded	*1 tablespoon mushroom ketchup (page 14)*
1-inch piece gingerroot, shredded	*14 ounces ramen noodles*
1 scallion, finely sliced	*1 1/2 cups cubed firm tofu*
1/4 cups cubed firm tofu	
6 cups vegetable stock	*2 ounces fresh watercress*
2 ounces green beans	*Soy sauce, to serve*
1 carrot, cut into matchsticks	

Put the daikon, ginger, and scallion in three small serving bowls.

Bring the stock to a boil in a saucepan and blanch the beans for 2 minutes. Remove with a slotted spoon and set aside. Blanch the carrot matchsticks for 1 minute only, remove with a slotted spoon, and set aside. Flavor the stock with the mushroom ketchup.

Cook the noodles in plenty of boiling water according to the package directions. Drain.

Pile the noodles in the serving bowls. Divide the beans, carrot, tofu cubes, and watercress between the bowls. Ladle in the hot stock, and serve immediately, accompanied by the scallion, ginger, daikon, and soy sauce to be added to taste.

BASIL NOODLES WITH BAKED TOMATOES

A whole handful of fresh basil is used in this dish, not just a sprinkling. As a result, the flavor just explodes!

8 ounces plum tomatoes	*1/2 bunch (1 oz) fresh basil*
1 teaspoon salt	*2 teaspoons olive oil*
1 teaspoon sugar	*Salt and freshly ground black pepper*
8 ounces egg thread noodles	*Parmesan shavings, to serve*

Preheat the oven to 350°F/180°C. Halve the tomatoes and toss them with the salt and sugar. Spread them out in a baking tray and bake for about 1 hour or until they collapse. Let cool.

Cook the noodles in boiling water for 3–4 minutes or according to the package directions. Drain well and keep warm.

Put the basil in a blender or food processor and blend in enough olive oil to make a paste. Add this to the noodles and stir until they are evenly coated. Season generously with black pepper and salt to taste.

Spoon the tomatoes over the noodles. Sprinkle with Parmesan shavings, and serve.

TEMPURA SOBA

The ultimate in contrasts: soba noodles in broth topped with tempura—deep-fried vegetables in a crisp, light batter. A dipping sauce is served alongside, for the tempura.

1 carrot, cut into strips about	*1 cup sweet potato cut into*
3/8 x 1 1/4 inches	*3/4 inch dice*
1/4 cup broccoli florets	*Vegetable oil for deep-frying*
2 ounces green beans	*All-purpose flour for coating*
1 zucchini, cut into strips about	*8 ounces soba noodles*
3/8 x 1 1/4 inches	*5 cups dashi broth*
1 cup button mushrooms	

FOR THE DIPPING SAUCE	*FOR THE BATTER*
5 tablespoons mirin	*1 egg yolk*
5 tablespoons soy sauce	*Scant 2 cups ice-cold water*
3 tablespoons dried bonito flakes	*1 1/2 cups all-purpose flour*
	Pinch of baking soda

First make the dipping sauce. Bring the mirin to a boil in a small saucepan and boil to reduce by half. Stir in the soy sauce and bonito flakes, and return to a boil. Immediately remove from the heat and strain. Transfer the sauce to a serving dish and set aside.

Blanch the carrot strips in boiling water for 1 minute, refresh under cold running water, and drain well.

Prepare all the remaining vegetables, then make the batter. Stir the egg yolk with the cold water. Sift in the flour and baking soda and stir until the batter is smooth.

Heat oil in a wok or deep-fat fryer to 350°F/180°C. Coat the vegetables lightly in flour. Working in batches, dip them into the batter and then immediately deep-fry in the hot oil for about 1 minute. Drain on paper towels and keep warm in a low oven.

Cook the noodles in the boiling dashi broth for 4 minutes or according to the package directions. Drain, reserving the broth.

Pile the noodles into the serving bowls and ladle in the broth. Top each bowl with a few deep-fried vegetables. Serve immediately, accompanied by the dipping sauce for the vegetables.

RECIPE INDEX

First published in the United States of America in 1996 by
Rizzoli International Publications, Inc.

300 Park Avenue South, New York, NY 10010

First published in Great Britain in 1996 by
George Weidenfeld & Nicolson Limited
The Orion Publishing Group

ISBN 0-8478-1939-6

LC 95-72945

Designed by Design Revolution, Brighton, England

Printed and bound in Italy